OverJoyed!

Women OF FAITH

OverJoyed!

Devotions to Tickle Your Fancy and Strengthen Your Faith

Patsy Clairmont · Barbara Johnson
Marilyn Meberg · Luci Swindoll
Sheila Walsh · Thelma Wells

with Janet Kobobel Grant

ZondervanPublishingHouse
Grand Rapids, Michigan

A Division of HarperCollinsPublishers

OverJoyed!
Copyright © 1999 by Women of Faith, Inc.

Requests for information should be addressed to:
🏭 ZondervanPublishingHouse
Grand Rapids, Michigan 49530

Library of Congress Cataloging-in-Publication Data

OverJoyed!: 60 devotions to tickle your fancy and strengthen your faith/
    Patsy Clairmont . . . [et al.].
        p.   cm.
        ISBN: 0-310-22653-8 (hardcover)
    1. Women—Prayer-books and devotions—English. I. Clairmont,
Patsy.
BV4844.O84   1998
242'.643-dc 21   98-11682
                                                                CIP

Scripture quotations are from:

The Holy Bible, New International Version (NIV), © 1973, 1984 by the
International Bible Society. Used by permission of Zondervan Publishing
House;

New American Standard Bible (NASB), © 1960, 1977 by the Lockman
Foundation;

The Message, © 1993, 1994, 1995 by Eugene H. Peterson;

The Living Bible (TLB), © 1971 by Tyndale House Publishers.

This edition printed on acid-free paper and meets the American National
Standards Institute Z39.48 standard.

Printed in the United States of America

---

99 00 01 02 03 04 /❖ DC/ 10 9 8 7 6 5 4 3

Contents

✗♥✗♥✗♥✗♥✗♥✗♥✗♥✗♥✗♥✗♥✗♥✗♥

Part One

Over the Top: Flamboyant as We Wanna Be

Part Two

Move Over Misery: Move in Joy

Part Three

Undergirded: For the Overtired, Overloaded, and Overwhelmed

Part Four

Turning Over a New Leaf: And Finding the Joy

Part Five

Over and Over: Thoughts Worth Repeating

Part Six
Overalls: Covered in Righteousness

Part Seven
Over and Above What We Dreamed: God's Surprises

Over the Top

Flamboyant as We Wanna Be

Rats Giggle

Marilyn Meberg

If it is encouraging, let him encourage; if it is contributing
to the needs of others, let him give generously.

ROMANS 12:8

This morning I read this headline in the newspaper: "Rats Giggle, Tests Find." A researcher at Bowling Green State University found that rats are not only playful but they also love to be tickled. Apparently, scientists have known that about rats for some time, but psychobiologist Jaak Pankseep is doing a study on rats that attempts to track the biological origins of joy.

What I found fascinating was Jaak's description of how to make a rat giggle. He says, "It's quite easy. Rats are small, of course, but it's really no different than using your fingertips as if you were tickling a child. You get the most laughter at the nape of the neck."*

In case you, like I, wondered how in the world one would know if a rat is laughing, their sounds are recorded by using "bat detectors," sophisticated instruments that register high-pitched sounds humans cannot hear. "When a bunch of rats are all tickled at the same time," Pankseep says, "it sounds like a children's playground at recess."

Of all creatures on the earth, in my mind rats would be the least likely candidates to take giggle breaks. I have found myself smiling about that fact all day. The article has also caused me to spin off on a reverie concerning "least likely" humans I have either known or briefly encountered whom I wondered if a smile, giggle, or laugh ever escaped their frozen lips.

Los Angeles Times, May 4, 1998, Section A.

Eighty-year-old Mrs. Davidson, about whom I write in another devotional in this book, falls into the frozen-lip category. Yet, as a child, I found her fascinating. A good part of my fascination was undoubtedly that she would occasionally shout out disagreements during my father's preaching. I, on the other hand, wasn't even allowed to interrupt during second-grade reading group, much less Dad's sermons. I was tremendously envious of all she got away with.

Since she lived within walking distance of our parsonage, I loved dropping in on her. She never seemed particularly glad to see me; instead, she appeared indifferent to my visits. She had an acre of land on which she housed a number of chickens, a goat named Bert, and a cow also named Bert. (I never thought to question the duplication of names or the appropriateness of a cow's having such a moniker.) Mrs. Davidson was always puttering around outside doing various little chores, and I trailed along behind her chatting and trying in vain to engage her in some way.

One night at supper my parents quizzed me about why I liked visiting Mrs. Davidson. I think they were concerned she might find me a nuisance or that she might hurt my feelings. I told my parents I liked her animals and loved the smell of her few bales of alfalfa, but more than that, I wanted to make her laugh. Both parents put down their forks and looked kindly at me.

"Honey," my father said, "I've never even seen Mrs. Davidson smile, much less laugh."

One of the things we did as a small family of three was make various bets. Dad always was betting my mother about some academic subject which he was sure he was right about only to find he was totally wrong. That never seemed to squelch his enthusiasm, however, and the bets continued as long as they lived.

Thinking I might get in on the betting game, I said to my parents, "I'll bet I can get Mrs. Davidson to laugh before I'm in the third grade!" Rising to the challenge, they agreed and said they hoped I won the bet. Mom asked what kind of payoff I wanted.

"French toast for breakfast every Saturday morning for six weeks," I said without hesitation.

For at least a month I tried every conceivable thing I could think of to make Mrs. Davidson laugh. I told her jokes, I told her all the bad things Lester Courtney did in school, I even did acrobatics for her. No response.

Then one day, as I was heading up the path toward her messy property, I was attempting to perfect my imitation of how Mr. Brownell walked. Mr. Brownell had caught his leg in a threshing machine at some point in his life, and the accident resulted in the most memorable walk I'd ever seen. Whenever his weight landed on his bad leg, his whole body would veer dangerously out of balance. But somehow the flapping of his arms caused him to catapult in the opposite direction until everything appeared to be back in order. His head moved in perfect rhythm to all this disjointedness. It was quite a feat.

I had been working on this imitation for some time purely for my own sense of accomplishment. My efforts were interrupted by the sound of what could be likened to a donkey's braying. It grew louder and louder until finally I located where the noise was coming from. Mrs. Davidson was leaning against the side of her chicken house, laughing. She laughed so long, so loud, and so hard it made me a little nervous. It seemed to me making that much noise could kill a person.

"Well, Mr. Brownell," she finally gasped, "how nice of you to visit me," and then she went into another braying episode.

When I triumphantly announced to my parents that I had won the bet, they were concerned the laughter had come at the expense of another's misfortune. I explained that I had been working on the walk for weeks but never to be used for Mrs. Davidson, and in fact, I had no idea she saw me until I heard her laugh. Apparently convinced that my heart was not cruel, I was rewarded with French toast every Saturday for six weeks.

I still find myself wanting to make people smile or laugh. It's a little game I play with myself when experiencing a gloomy waitress, bank teller, store clerk, or any other frozen-lipped personage. Scripture states that we are to be encouragers and to meet other's needs. What a fun way to take that verse seriously and make an effort to meet the "joy needs" of those around us. It sure beats tickling rats.

"Lord, as you increase our joy, may we make an effort to spread that joy around us in your name. Amen."

Hair Today ...
Gone Tomorrow
Sheila Walsh

✗❤✗❤✗❤✗❤✗❤✗❤✗❤✗❤✗❤✗❤✗❤

Even to your old age and gray hairs I am he, I am he who
will sustain you. I have made you and I will carry you; I
will sustain you and I will rescue you.

ISAIAH 46:4

If God counts every hair that falls from our heads, he must
be exhausted counting mine with all the abuse I ladle out
to my head of hair. I think some women have an extra gene
called the "hair coloring gene." We poor souls honestly believe
we can buy a little box of color in a drugstore, and we will
look like the woman pictured on the box. Never happens!

But that doesn't stop me. Oh, no! I march on down the road
of hair destruction in search of that elusive perfect shade.

My first foray into this bleak and unforgiving world was with
a shade called "warm coffee brown." *Sounds lovely,* I thought.
I like coffee ... This will be good.

It turned out black. Boot-polish black. Elvira black. A-crow-
died-on-your-head black. *Never mind,* I consoled myself. *I'll
try again.*

And so I did with "golden ash."

"How emotionally evocative," I mused. "I'll be like a tree
in the fall, all shades of gold and amber."

Well, I was half right. I did look like a tree ... in the middle of June. It was green, green, green.

I pressed on. Next I ordered what was described as "luxuri-
ous hair" by a woman on television with big hair. I thought, *I*

can't go wrong with this. I just attach these hairpieces under my own hair for full, flowing, glorious locks.

When I opened the box the contents looked like a row of dead hamsters. I tried them on and had to admit I resembled a rather sad-looking cocker spaniel.

But the greatest damage I've ever done to my hair happened when I was eighteen years old and just about to leave my little Scottish town for university in the big city of London. I was very excited and wanted to look hip. I had long, silky hair, which I decided was too old fashioned. I needed a new look. So I bought a *Vogue* magazine and studied all the pictures. One model had hair that was cut in layers and softly permed. She looked beautiful.

"Do you like this hairstyle, Mom?" I asked one evening after dinner.

"It looks lovely, Sheila," she replied. "Why?"

"I'm thinking of having this done before I go to London."

She begged me not to. She begged me to wait and have it done in a London salon. But I wanted to arrive as the new me. I took the magazine picture to a small salon in my hometown of Ayr and asked one of the stylists if she could do it.

"Oh, sure, lassie. It'll be lovely!"

I decided not to look until she was finished. I wanted a big surprise. I got one. At first I thought something was wrong with the mirror, but then I realized I was looking at my head. I can't adequately depict the fright that was me. My hair was layered different lengths on each side. It was also fried. I looked as if I'd stuck my wet finger in an electric socket. I numbly paid and began to walk down the road.

I talked to myself as I went. "It's not as bad as you think. It'll be better when it's washed. Christ may return today."

Just at that moment I spotted my mom and my brother, who were waiting for me outside a coffee shop. Stephen was laughing so hard he was clinging to a pole to try to hold himself up.

My poor mother was attempting to make him stand up and behave, but her efforts just caused him to laugh harder. He ended up lying on the sidewalk.

I was eighteen then. I'm forty-two now, and thankfully I've learned how to handle my hair. One other thing I've learned is that my worth to God has nothing to do with how I look or feel. He is committed to me on my good hair days and on my bad hair days. And when I make a fright of my spiritual life— even committing errors that seem "permanent"—Jesus can wash them away. He is eager to do so and will never laugh, regardless of how ridiculous I look.

If today, as you look in the mirror, you wonder if this is a face only a mother could love, remember, it's a face a *Father* loves!

"Thank you, Father, for loving me through all my fragile, silly days. Thank you for holding me close to your heart, under your wing. Amen."

Sticky Situation

Patsy Clairmont

When Luci invited me to join her and some other gals to tour Mrs. Grossman's Paper Company, which specializes in stickers, I was tickled. I had been casually using stickers in my sometimes journal (sometimes I write in it, sometimes I don't), and I often affixed stickers to the backs of envelopes.

Now, Luci is a sticker artisan. Using stickers, she creatively expresses herself in ways that make you giggle and bless your heart. So when Luci invited me to join the group for a day of sticker investigating, the childlike part of my heart perked up.

We six giddy gals arrived at Mrs. Grossman's company to find Andrea Grossman cheerfully waiting to receive us. Her enthusiastic greeting and introductions to her staff were just the beginning of a delightful experience. Later we would highlight this day in our journals—with stickers, of course.

We began with a tour of the facilities. I would have never guessed all that is involved in designing and manufacturing teensy-weensy stick-ums. As a sticker starts at one end of the machine that prints it, the paper is blank, but it comes out the other end colorfully arrayed (sort of like me in front of my morning mirror). The company produces tiny, medium, and mega-sized stickers (sort of like the sizes of clothes in my closet). Some stickers sparkle, some are luminous, and some appear dimensional. (Sort of like, uh, my personality? Hmm, perhaps not.) During the tour we passed store racks filled with rolls of sticker characters, holidays, animals, children, toys, houses . . .

All day I had the most delicious desire to break into a skip. Well, actually I did. When Andrea invited us to visit the racks and take what we wanted, I felt like a child with a balloon being blown up inside of her. I was about to burst as I skipped my way to the racks, which beckoned like candy counters crowded with yummy choices. *Yippee!* I wanted to shout, but I stifled that cry and tried to behave like an adult (what a stretch).

I kept reminding myself not to be too generous with myself. But as I filled my bag, and it began to overflow, I knew "myself" was losing control. No wonder we give children guidelines. The more I took the more I wanted. No wonder *God* gives us guidelines! Finally, I mentally and physically dragged myself away from the enticing racks and headed for the van. On the two-and-a-half-hour trip back to the hotel, we all tried to organize our gazillion stickers while we giggled and chortled over our day.

My companions were equally amazed at the range of emotions they had felt. We had all moved from goodie-goodie to grabby-grabby. We went from gratitude to greed back to gratitude. The childish phrase, "It's mine, it's mine," kept bounding through my brain when I would reach for yet another roll of stickers. At one point during our rampage, our friend Judy collapsed on the floor in giggles, bedecked in sticker streamers.

Mrs. Grossman's generosity (Luci will fill you in later) was greatly appreciated by all of us. She gave us a chance to feel like kids again. Whee! What a gift, and what a reminder. We can all benefit from those spontaneous, childlike moments in which we are thrilled with life's offerings. But an unguarded, childish heart can leave one needy and greedy regardless of age.

How long has it been since you skipped? Slurped Popsicles? Hopscotched? Played jacks? Released a balloon? Give yourself permission to take a break and celebrate. Then press on into childlike faith and enjoy the bounty of delights he has provided us.

"Daddy God, thank you for applauding our being childlike, for it's such fun and so restorative—not just as we play ballerina on our tiptoes, but as we, in childlike spontaneity, reach up to you. May we learn to be deliberately generous in extending opportunities to others to know your parental care. As we stuff our bags full of your goodies (peace, patience, love, joy), may we then share them lavishly. Thank you for always sticking by us. Amen."

The Infamous Bra
Thelma Wells

Do not lie to each other, since you have taken off your
old self with its practices and have put on the new self,
which is being renewed in knowledge in the image of its
Creator. Here there is no Greek or Jew, circumcised or
uncircumcised, barbarian, Scythian, slave or free, but
Christ is all, and is in all.

COLOSSIANS 3:9–11

Ladies come to the Women of Faith conferences with all
kinds of issues and situations. Some come with their own
agendas. And a few of them seem to be a little over-the-top.
You know, their compass seems to be headed in the opposite
direction from the rest of the world.

That's the impression TJ gave at a conference attended by
fifteen thousand women earlier this year. While other women
were applauding the singers and speakers, TJ waved a white,
size 44D, lace brassiere in the air, as high as she could.

She had come with a busload of ladies from her church, but
some of these fellow travelers were embarrassed by her unusual
interaction with those on the stage. Her pastor's wife vowed
to take that thing away from TJ. But she wasn't giving it up easily. Instead of handing over the bra, she swirled it in the air and
yelled "Hallelujah" at the top of her voice. All her parish pals
could do was act as if they didn't know her.

I met TJ when she ran up to my book table during a break
with the big bra in hand and enthusiastically insisted, "Sign my
bra! Please sign my bra! I want you to sign it right here!"

I looked at her in shock. I have signed T-shirts, books, audio-cassette and CD covers, brochures, programs, bumblebee pin cards, earring holders, postcards, and tablecloths. But bras, never. I thought, *If TJ has the nerve to sling a bra around in front of thousands of women and then ask me to autograph it, that's the least I can do*. I signed it, "My cup runneth over!"

Okay, so you think my compass is as misdirected as TJ's. I saw it all as great fun. TJ certainly seemed to be having a good time.

That autographing moment was the beginning of a wonderful relationship that has included spiritual growth and renewal for me. When I returned home from the conference, TJ telephoned and asked me to speak at her church for Multicultural Celebration Day. She said she had attended the Women of Faith conference asking God to direct her to the person the Lord wanted as speaker for the celebration day. She was convinced God had led her to ask me.

I agreed to be that speaker. During the many conversations with TJ that followed, I discovered she loves the Lord with all her heart. She has a passion for winning the lost to Christ and has compassion for hurting people. Her heartfelt urge for people to be united was evidenced by her consistent prayers for unity of the races, understanding among the denominations, and reconciliation of people's differences in every aspect of life. Her faith in God was evidenced by her determination to follow through on what she believed he had led her to do with this conference.

Sometimes TJ would call my answering service in the middle of the night to leave a word of encouragement for my staff and me to receive the following day. She introduced me to her mother and her husband over the telephone, and I recognized a family commitment to loyalty and harmony that could exist only among God-loving people.

The theme for the daylong celebration TJ organized was "Fresh oil—a new and fresh anointing uniting the body of Christ." And the day truly was a time of reconciliation for the body of Christ in that Methodist church in Arkansas. Along with learning to sing, "What a Friend We Have in Jesus" in Japanese, we were enlightened, encouraged, and inspired by representatives from Scotland, Russia, Puerto Rico, Mexico, Germany, Switzerland, Israel, Spain, Romania, Bulgaria, Korea, Poland, as well as by Native Americans and African Americans.

As the keynote speaker, I explained that every culture represented there had roots stemming from the flood survivors—Mr. and Mrs. Noah, Mr. and Mrs. Shem, Mr. and Mrs. Japheth, and Mr. and Mrs. Ham. But the most powerful time was after I spoke and the charge for reconciliation was given by TJ. We all sang, "Let there be peace on earth, and let it begin with me," as we went to each other with love, hugging and holding each other and saying words of apology or comfort. At that moment, all of us seemed to realize that we are sisters and brothers, valuable members of the human race regardless of origin or ethnic background.

Sharing communion was a beautiful sight. All the cultures represented were around the altar tearing pieces off a loaf of bread and dipping into the same cup of wine.

Just think, if I hadn't signed that infamous bra, I might have missed the opportunity to participate in the most prayed-up, planned-up, and thought-out day of cultural togetherness of my life. And I learned that not all people who act a little over-the-top should be labeled "off sides" just because they do things differently from the norm. You really can't judge a book by its cover. You have to look inside to see how the pages read.

Have you missed the opportunity of a lifetime because you thought the person who offered it was the sort who would use a size 44D bra as a flag? I'm not suggesting you throw caution to the wind. But I am suggesting that if someone presents you with an unusual opportunity, check your gut feeling before you write it off. God gave us intuition that can work for us when we let it. I don't suggest waving a brassiere at a conference, however. Leave that for TJ.

"Master, you did some unusual things during your walk here on earth. People thought you were a bit strange. Teach us to love everybody regardless of their race, ethnic origin, religion, geographic location, educational status, financial ability, social standing, personality, or physical ability. And when we want to ignore or move away from people we don't understand, help us to listen to our instincts and not to miss out on some of the best blessings—even when they come in unusual packages. Amen."

Too Huge

Luci Swindoll

✗♥✗♥✗♥✗♥✗♥✗♥✗♥✗♥✗♥✗♥
Finally, brothers, whatever is true, whatever is noble,
whatever is right, whatever is pure, whatever is lovely,
whatever is admirable—if anything is excellent or
praiseworthy—think about such things.

PHILIPPIANS 4:8

I'll never forget Joanne DeGraw. She was unique, exceptional, and charming. Our friendship was extraordinary. When she died of cancer, which she battled bravely for seventeen years, something in me wanted to die, too.

I loved Joanne. Texan by birth, she was highly educated, married to an attorney, and the mother of two. A former resident of France, she loved literature, art, theater, and music. She was an unparalleled interior designer.

When we met, I was renting an apartment. She promptly designed a house for me and said, if it ever became a reality, she would like to do the decorating. I was thrilled, and almost immediately we made plans. Although she died before I had my dream house, she lived to shepherd me through the process of purchasing furniture and appointments I'd need for my home.

Joanne had a great sense of humor in spite of the severity of her physical condition. Whether we were discussing the latest book we had read, an opera we had seen together, the Scripture, her children, or my home-decorating project, she injected her flair for the funny in her sweet Southern twang.

I remember my excitement over finding a group of six teeny lamp shades I wanted to use on a chandelier in my dining room. They seemed perfect. When I showed them to Joanne, she said,

"Why, Luci, those will never do!" Surprised, I asked why not. "They are too huge!" she responded. I couldn't imagine how anything less than two inches high could be too huge, but I trusted her judgment. On that, and everything else, she knew what she was doing.

A year before Joanne died, I visited her for four days. On the first morning, when I awakened, I found a pot of coffee, a gorgeous china cup, and this note on her personalized stationery: *Good morning, dear Luci, good morning to you. I am looking forward to spending a whole day with you. Enjoy the library in the peace of the morning, and the coffee while it's hot!*

During that precious time together we spent long days in front of a roaring fire, talking and laughing, reading aloud, eating, cooking, and chatting about dreams, joys, and regrets. On the third day she received the report that tumors for which she was being treated had, in fact, grown and metastasized into the liver. She hung up the phone, cried a few minutes, told me what had happened, and asked me to pray with her. Then, out of the blue, she said, "I know a great bookstore in Grass Valley, Luci. Let's go over there and see what damage we can do, okay?" And away we went! The seriousness of her diagnosis didn't set the tone for our day; her indomitable spirit did. In spite of our sadness, the day was sweet, fun, and memorable.

Joanne could have made her suffering a time of emotional torment for herself and anguish for her loved ones, but she didn't. She decided instead to accept the path God gave her with courage, grace, and humor. Without denying her reality, she chose to think on what was excellent and praiseworthy.

When I look at the furniture she chose for the home I now own, I remember her joy of living and spirit of giving. I think, *Joanne DeGraw, your spirit was just too huge for this old world!*

Should you encounter bad news today, look within yourself. You'll find God's Spirit, which will enable you to accept graciously that which has been handed to you. Think on those parts of life that are lovely. For even in our saddest days, God is under the sorrow, holding us up.

"Help me, Lord, to think on those things that bring honor to you. Give me joy in my circumstances so that my life will bring others joy instead of sadness. Amen."

Dream On

Barbara Johnson

His divine power has given us everything we need for life
and godliness through our knowledge of him who called
us by his own glory and goodness.

2 Peter 1:3

"Easy instructions, yeah right," said the elderly lady, shaking her head at a jumble of wood, paper, and string. "Another nice, windy day gone to waste," she added with a sigh.

Just then a young man passing by noticed her dilemma. He suggested they pool their wits and try to assemble the kite.

"You go ahead," the lady said. "I've used up all my wits today."

Twenty minutes later, up went the kite. Like a yellow butterfly it caught the wind, dipping, tacking, soaring. The lady gave a whoop as she tugged on the string. "You know, I looked out this morning and said, 'Mary, do it, just do it.' And here I am!"

Recently someone challenged me to make a list of fifty things I want to do before I die. That wasn't hard at all. The hard part is deciding *how* to do them. Most of the things on my list are like flying a kite—easy to dream of but complicated to put together.

Then I thought, *Does that really matter? The important thing is to know what I want and then to try.* When you "just do it," God gets behind you and lends his grace or sometimes a miracle or two, like the young man who came along when the lady was ready to give up.

Often the best place to start is doing that which is right in your lap. Is it a child to raise? A feud to mend? A field to hoe?

As Francis of Assisi worked in his garden one day, someone asked him, "What would you do if the world were going to end tomorrow?"

"I'd go right on pulling these weeds," Francis answered.

Sometimes a dream is simple—maybe just laughing more. Or rising early to see the sunrise once a week. Or watching it set over the Pacific once in a lifetime. It might be telling someone special that you love him or her. You don't have to ride a camel before you die. You might not want to climb Mt. Everest or sail on the Mediterranean. You don't need to swim the deepest river or cross the widest desert.

The sweetest bliss is in taking the next step, even if it leads to your favorite coffee shop or candy store. The best thing is to be there, where you are, for yourself, the people you love, and the people who love you. Think about those things that bring you joy. Go out and look for them.

But don't forget, you may encounter on your journey those who need you to help them put together their kites so they can realize their dreams, too. It takes so few minutes to make someone's day. A friend may need nothing more than a listening ear. When you do the talking, serve up your words soft and sweet, for you never know when you may have to eat them.

At times women become so engrossed in taking care of the needs of others that they don't take a moment to think about their own. Maybe you can set aside a half hour this week to write down your dreams. Go ahead and elaborate. Dream on. Then write a prayer committing them to the Lord.

For most of us, relationships will be at the heart of our dreams. And if we have children, they will probably play a big part. Our desires are bound up with the people we love. But it's okay to want nothing more than to fly a kite. Just tie your dreams to your kite's tail and hang on tight. Anything can happen!

"Father, I want to feel your wind at my back, your breeze filling my sails, your sunshine on my shoulder. I give you my

wildest, most colorful dreams. I believe you gave them to me first. I want them in your time and your place. Prepare me to meet others who are making their dreams come true. I'll look out for opportunities to put someone's kite together. Amen."

I Think I Can, I Think I Can
Sheila Walsh

❤✖❤✖❤✖❤✖❤✖❤✖❤✖❤✖❤✖❤✖❤✖❤✖❤✖❤✖

Therefore, I urge you, brothers, in view of God's mercy, to
offer your bodies as living sacrifices, holy and pleasing to
God—this is your spiritual act of worship. Do not conform
any longer to the pattern of this world, but be transformed
by the renewing of your mind. Then you will be able to
test and approve what God's will is—his good, pleasing
and perfect will.

ROMANS 12:1–2

Nothing is worse than trying to squeeze yourself into something that doesn't fit. Just ask my friend Marlene! She
was one of my bridesmaids and had to go through that awful
ritual of being inflicted with a bridesmaid's dress. Because it was
a winter wedding, I chose hunter green velvet dresses. Nancy,
my matron of honor, lived in England so I had to guess her
size and send it over hoping for the best. My other two bridesmaids were being fitted in Charleston so they were taken care
of, but Marlene was another matter.

She was so busy she didn't have time to be measured for
the dress but was fairly confident that she would wear a certain size. (Size withheld out of desire for continued friendship.)
I told her the assistant in the store said a person should order
a size larger than normal since bridesmaid dresses are usually
cut small. But Marlene said no. I decided to order the larger size
anyway and cut off the label. This seemed like a brain wave
until it arrived, and Marlene asked me why I'd cut off the label.

"You ordered the bigger size, didn't you?" she said.

"I cannot lie," I replied. "Just try it on."

She came out of her bedroom in a few moments with a stunned
look on her face. "It's too small!" she cried. "I can't zip it up."

We didn't have time to order a new one. We were stuck.

"Well, you just can't ever eat again; that's all," I said.

"Don't worry," she replied. "I have a plan." When Marlene said she had a plan, you can never tell what might happen.

The big day arrived. All the bridesmaids were dressing in my room, and sure enough, Marlene slipped into her attire and looked beautiful.

"How did you do it?" I whispered.

"I'll tell you later," she said.

Finally, we had a few moments together at the reception. "You have to let me in on your secret," I said.

"I was wrapped," she replied.

"You were what?" I asked.

"Wrapped like a turkey at Thanksgiving," she said proudly. "I went to a beauty salon every day and was trussed like a bird for the oven to melt me into the svelte figure before you."

We still laugh about that when we get together. I'm touched by the lengths my friend went to for my wedding day, above and beyond the call of duty. I know that what she went through was uncomfortable and unnatural.

But I wonder how often we do that to our souls as we try to fit into this world. The mold that this world would like to squeeze us into is an ill-fitting one. Instead, Christ calls us to be transformed in how we think, and to evaluate the messages that are sent to us every day through the television screen, on the billboards, and in the mall. We don't have to pull our hearts and souls in to accommodate this ill-fitting outfit that our culture would have us wear. Instead, we are free to be just us, renewed hearts and all.

"Lord Jesus, thank you for setting me free from the tight clothes of this world to be dressed in your righteousness instead. Amen."

You-nique and Chosen
Thelma Wells

❌❤❌❤❌❤❌❤❌❤❌❤❌❤❌❤❌❤❌❤❌❤❌❤
For you created my inmost being; you knit me together in
my mother's womb. I praise you because I am fearfully
and wonderfully made.

PSALM 139:13–14

God made you an original; don't die a copy. In the late seventies, a friend gave me a motto I use in all the sessions I present, whether Christian or secular: "In Christ, you can be the best of what and whom you want to BEE!" I also tell people about the bumblebee I wear every day, everywhere I go.

According to aeronautical science, the bumblebee can't fly. Its body is too heavy, and its wings are too shallow. But the bumblebee doesn't know it can't fly. So it flies around doing what God chose for it to do, pollinating plants. It does so without considering its limitations.

BEE aware that you, too, have talent, skill, aptitude, and ability that are you-niquely yours. No two people sing, dance, paint, speak, organize, manage, or teach just alike. When God made us, he made us special. We can be the best of what and who we want to BEE—and only God knows what our limitations are.

When I had my first child, I didn't understand about you-niqueness. So I tried to clone myself. I wanted to make my daughter in my image. But her personality was so different. She liked to stay in her room and read. She wasn't outgoing and didn't smile often. I thought she hated people. I would take her places and introduce her to people. Her response would be a cold, "Hi."

For years I put up with this attitude until one day it wore me down. I had introduced my twelve-year-old daughter to someone, and she gave her same non-nonchalant, non-person-ality, non-smiling, unfriendly, "Hi." When we got back in the car, I verbally went for her jugular. I had a nervous breakdown on her for about forty-five minutes.

"What is wrong with you? Why are you so cold and non-responsive? Why don't you act like you have home training? Do you hate people so much you don't even want to meet them?" I went on asking questions, and then I made another round in which I answered them myself.

When I finally finished my tirade, I noticed I hadn't moved her one bit. In fact, she just said, "Mama, I love you. But I'm not you. I don't even want to be like you."

What? Did she say she didn't want to be like me? What's wrong with me? How dare she; I'm a wonderful person. I decided to get my feelings hurt. (Notice I said, "I decided." Nobody can hurt your feelings without your cooperation.) I was so hurt I didn't even want to feed her, but I had to. After all, she was still my responsibility.

At first I couldn't rationally think about her comments. But, as I began to seriously consider what she was trying to com-municate, I understood she was saying, "Mother, I am my own person. I have my unique personality and ask that you respect my individuality."

I started to pay more attention to her actions and discovered that reading, analyzing, and thinking through situations were things she was interested in. People were important, but more important to her were answers to questions she could find in books, magazines, and journals. In fact, when I would take her to a grocery store or drugstore, she would stop at the maga-zine rack and would remain there until I was ready to leave. This very child has become the analytical, legal mind of my business. God made her unique.

If you have more than one child, you see the differences in them. We have three children. My middle child has my per-sonality. He likes to make people laugh, obviously loves life, is a relational person. He also looks like his mother . . . a good-looking man! Our youngest child is more serious and quiet. She is patient, kind, tender, and compassionate.

When I disciplined child #1, she wanted to know: "Why? How many? How come? What do you mean by that?" And she expected clear-cut answers.

When I disciplined child #2, he would hug and kiss me and tell me he would never repeat the offense. Sure. Give him ten minutes, and he would be right back at it.

With child #3, all I had to do was to look at her with motherly anger. She would start to cry because she never wanted to hurt or disappoint me.

Three different people with the same mother and father, but all unique and chosen by God.

You might appear to be different—or even strange—to some people. But remember, God made you in his image for his glory. Use your uniqueness to edify people and glorify God. Capitalize on the abilities God has given you. Don't expect other people to be like you or to always understand you. They're busy being uniquely themselves.

"Father, you make trillions of people, each with unique abilities, skills, thought patterns, talents, and personality. Each of us is different in so many ways. Thank you that our uniqueness can be linked to other people's uniqueness so harmony can exist in relationships, on our jobs, and in the church. Help us to accept other people's uniqueness as a God-given opportunity to blend and bless. Amen."

What a Guy
Marilyn Meberg

As a bridegroom rejoices over his bride, so will your God
rejoice over you.

ISAIAH 62:5

*E*ight years ago today, as I write this devotional, Ken
Meberg burst through the portals of heaven looking, I'm
sure, for something that needed to be organized. He was a wonderfully competent guy who kept me aware of time and place.

I knew what time it was and where I was; I just didn't think
about it much. To this day, I live in the moment and frequently
find it amazing one ought to be aware of things that aren't in
the moment. Understandably, that characteristic was an occasional burden to my long-suffering husband, but his patience
and creativity ultimately set me on a more balanced track.

When we were first married, my car would occasionally run
out of gas. I knew intellectually that a car runs on fuel that must
be replenished from time to time. But on the other hand, once
the car had been gassed up, I was surprised it wouldn't stay full.
The same inefficient law of nature extended to groceries. How
on earth could we be out of Tabasco sauce; I bought some once.

One of the greatest challenges I contributed to Ken's life was
during the third year of our marriage. We decided to obtain a
credit card to help us in time of need (which happened to be
at the end of each month). I found the card a wonderfully handy
benefactor and began to avail myself of its generosity. My usual
illogic applied to this card. I didn't seem to remember that what
was purchased yesterday needed to be paid for today. Mercy,
other things are going on right now.

Ken had mentioned the overuse of the card to me several times, and I had listened conscientiously at the moment. But, of course, that moment soon became past tense and ... well ... you know.

The doorbell rang one morning as one-year-old Jeff was dazzling me with his ability to lurch about the room without holding on to anything. (This action is commonly called "walking," but Jeff's movements were more accurately described as "lurching.") I opened the door to a stern-looking gentleman who asked if my name was Marilyn Meberg. After I owned up to that fact, he asked if he could please see my Bank of America card. That struck me as an odd request, but I innocently pulled it from my wallet, which was in proximity to the door. He asked if he could examine it. I mindlessly handed it to him. (Do not try this in your own home; only the professionally mindless are qualified to accomplish this feat.)

With a dramatic flourish, he pulled from his pocket a small pair of scissors and sliced the card in two. I stared at him in disbelief as he handed the two card pieces back to me. Turning on his heel he said, "That's what happens to card abusers!"

I stood rooted to the spot long after he disappeared down my walkway. Slowly, the scenario began to make sense. I started to grin, giggle, and finally guffaw. "Ken Meberg, you're good."

That evening, after Jeff had been bedded down, I joined Ken in the living room to read the paper. "Hey, Babe," I said to the newspaper that shielded his face from me. "I had a fun experience today."

"Really," he said tonelessly without lowering the paper.

"Yeah, a guy came to the front door and, based solely on my good credit, offered me a MasterCard with a $10,000 line of credit!"

Silence.

"Well, what do you think?"

Lowering his paper, Ken said with mischievous eyes, "That didn't happen."

"Well, how do you know?"

"'Cause that's not what I paid the guy to do!"

"You character! You really hired some guy with a suit and scissors to come to the front door and discipline me?"

"Yup," he said, picking up the paper.

"Where on earth did you find him?"

"I'm not telling; I might need him again!"

I miss Ken. I've wondered if he's keeping track of me from heaven and knows that I pay the bills, manage my finances, never run out of Tabasco sauce (which is easy because I don't use it), and keep gas in the car. Not only that, I have one credit card that I pay off at the end of each month. I think he would be proud of me. He contributed enormously to "growing me up," and I'm grateful.

In addition to preventing my life from having its edges tinged with chaos, Ken made me laugh. I never knew for sure what he was going to do or say, but at least once a day he would whiplash me with giggle inspirations. Like the time he gave me a birthday present in a huge box that progressed down to a tiny box. In the tiny box was a little gold charm for my bracelet. Guess what it was? A small pair of scissors. What a guy!

I wish the verse I selected for this devotional read, "As a bride rejoices over her bridegroom," because that's how I still feel about Ken. Our rejoicing over one another was a sweet gift. But God's rejoicing over us is even sweeter. We come into this relationship with all the flaws of a young bride but also with all the wonder, trust, and love. God, in turn, helps us to "grow up" in him. What a God!

"Lord, thank you for love and the richness it provides. Thank you for creating within us the capacity to express that love. Thank you that you model for us the kind of love that rejoices over one another and that your love never dies. Amen."

Move Over Misery

Move in Joy

✕❤✕❤✕❤✕❤✕❤✕❤✕❤✕❤✕❤✕❤✕❤

God Is Good Anyway

Barbara Johnson

I consider that our present sufferings are not worth
comparing with the glory that will be revealed in us.

ROMANS 8:18

We can't change these seven realities:

- Things are always changing.
- It rains on the just and the unjust.
- We are aging by the minute.
- The rules aren't fair.
- You can't please all people all the time.
- You can't heal another person's wounds.
- God is good anyway!

How often we need to be reminded that, regardless of our circumstances, God is constantly being good. And we're not the only ones who are forgetful. So is your best friend, the person in the pew in front of you, and the driver waiting in the car next to you at the stoplight.

But we're often reluctant to say, "God is good." We think our cup has to be full before we can share with somebody else. That's a big lie!

You don't have to be wealthy to start giving to the poor. You don't have to be perfectly organized to start giving of your time. You don't have to have a beautiful home to invite other people in. You don't have to be especially gifted to start making a difference in this world.

If you don't have it all together, join the club. You want to minister or start on the road to success? Use what you have. Begin with the things in your hands. As you give out of your emptiness or loneliness, the gifts flow back your way. It's a mystery, but when Jesus said, "Streams of living water will flow from within" (John 7:38), he was talking about a constant source of energy, love, and enthusiasm. So don't wait another minute to give from what you have; begin today. Do it anyway.

I know sometimes you feel too low to even take a baby step in the direction of someone else. But when your cup is so empty you wonder where the strength is going to come from . . . give, and it will be given to you.

Needing some spiritual CPR yourself? Wonder where you'll get enough spiritual oxygen to give to someone else? One time when I was feeling that way, I received a call from a friend whose husband was in intensive care. I didn't want to go out in the cold and the dark to be with her that night at the hospital. She didn't say, "I need you." She told me, "You don't have to come." I went anyway.

The hospital seemed so impersonal. White walls led down corridors of unmarked doors. Out-of-date magazines were sprawled across tables in the waiting area. I found my friend looking small and alone. When she saw me, tears flowed down her cheeks.

What can I possibly say to help her? I wondered. *Is there an appropriate Scripture to recite or prayer to repeat?*

Instead, I found myself starting to cry with my friend. Pretty soon we were hugging one another in that hospital room where a good man was dying.

The years have come and gone since that night, but still ringing in my heart is the Scripture, "Weep with them that weep" (Romans 12:15 KJV). Sometimes the right words are no words at all. Sometimes the best strength is no strength at all. Sometimes the way to minister to another human being is just to be present. Go anyway.

For each minute you think you have nothing to give, you lose sixty seconds of giving. For every hour you feel sorry for yourself, you lose sixty minutes to comfort another. For every day you wait to get going in the ministry to which God has called you, you lose twenty-four hours to bless the world.

Don't wait to start smiling if you're feeling blue. The Lord gives us a face, but it's up to us to provide the expression. And once the joy of giving gets in your system, it's bound to break out on your face.

You have a beautiful heart that is loved by the Lord Jesus. That is all you need. So don't wait until your troubles are behind you. The only person whose troubles are behind him is the schoolbus driver! Go to the phone and call a friend. Remind her that God is good. And if she doesn't agree right now, tell her that God is good anyway.

"Lord, keep me aware that this moment is the most precious moment of my life. Help me to use it to decide to reach out in your name. Amen."

A Joyful People
Marilyn Meberg

❌💗❌💗❌💗❌💗❌💗❌💗❌💗❌💗❌💗❌💗❌💗❌💗

You will go out in joy and be led forth in peace.

ISAIAH 55:12

Remember tight-lipped eighty-year-old Mrs. Davidson? She never appreciated my dad's easy laugh or his use of humor in the pulpit. She was given to spontaneous interruptions during many of his sermons. A colorful, unpredictable, and off-center little woman, her behavior and tongue couldn't be tamed. If Dad said something she didn't agree with, she would simply shout out, "Pastor, that's a bunch of hooey!"

He took it in stride and went on with his sermon. The people in our small congregation were used to her and didn't seem bothered. I was the one who eagerly anticipated her various outbursts, and my seven-year-old soul was deeply disappointed if a service didn't include Mrs. Davidson.

One Sunday, Mrs. Davidson was feeling especially vocal. Dad was barely into his sermon when she shouted, "Pastor, no one can laugh as much as you do and call himself a Christian."

Smiling, Dad pushed his sermon notes aside and spoke the rest of the hour about why joy needs to permeate every aspect of the Christian's life. Mrs. Davidson was uninspired and unmoved. The congregation, however, clapped heartily when he concluded.

Though I now recognize that Mrs. Davidson's behavior was probably rooted in dementia of some sort, her viewpoint has historical precedent. In the "Ordinance, Second Council of Constance," written in 1418, it says: "If any cleric or monk speaks jocular words such as provoke laughter, let him be anathema."

(I had to look up the word *anathema*; it means "a formal eccle-
siastical ban, curse, or excommunication." That's pretty serious.)
In the fourteenth century, my father would have been banned
as well as cursed for his use of humor in the pulpit.

Charles Baudelaire, an eighteenth-century French poet, said,
"Laughter is one of the most frequent symptoms of madness."

Isn't it amazing that laughter could have had such bad press
for so many centuries? I'm heartened by the words of the twen-
tieth-century C. S. Lewis, who wrote in *Reflections on the Psalms*,
"A little comic relief in a discussion does no harm however serious the topic may be. In my own experience the funniest things
have occurred in the gravest and most sincere conversations."
My kind of man!

In contrast to the leaders of the fourteenth-century Second Council of Constance, Scripture lauds joy as part of the
fruit of the Spirit. In fact, Acts 13:52 states, "The disciples were
filled with joy and with the Holy Spirit." It sounds as if both
joy and the filling of the Spirit happened at the same time;
joy must be important in God's eyes. Galatians 5:25 says, "Since
we live by the Spirit, let us keep in step with the Spirit." Does
that mean Christians who don't evidence joy aren't keeping
in step with the Spirit?

Now, I realize joy and laughter aren't the same. A person
can feel joy and not be laughing. But Acts 2:28 seems to
encourage more than just interior joy. "Thou hast made known
to me the ways of life; thou shalt make me full of joy with
thy countenance" (KJV).

I love a smiling countenance; I love even more a laughing
countenance. Something is so winsome in the sound and look
of laughter. It makes me want to join in even if I'm not sure
what the laughter is about. It just sounds fun, and sometimes
that's good enough!

I wonder if we Christians may need to pay more attention to
our countenance. I can't think of a more compelling witness of
my faith in God than to have my joy bubble over into laughter.

Incidentally, Mrs. Davidson continued her mirthless interruptions until the day she died at the age of eighty-six. She was hammering the last few boards onto her new chicken house when she dropped dead from a heart attack. Dad was the one who discovered her, still clutching her hammer. And while the congregation didn't miss her joyless editorials, knowing what she had missed in life left everyone a little bit sad.

"Lord, don't let me waste time being negative or joyless. May I seek to show evidence of the Holy Spirit's presence in my life, and may I give witness to those around me that God's people are joyful people. Amen."

Tub Talk

Thelma Wells

The LORD is my strength and my shield; my heart trusts in
him, and I am helped. My heart leaps for joy and I will
give thanks to him in song.

PSALM 28:7

God and I have some of the most interesting conversations
in the bathtub. Yes, I said "God and I." We talk to each
other all the time. Some call it prayer or meditation. But, whatever works for you, we were talking in the tub.

I was praying that he would reveal to me how to explain
his joy. Then I looked down at my hands splashing back and
forth in the water, and I saw something I had never noticed
before in that context—my diamond and gold jewelry.

On one hand I wore my platinum, antique, ornate, one-of-
a-kind diamond and baguette wedding band, which had been
on my finger for thirty-two years and had never needed repair-
ing. I had enhanced it by adding a gold rope band to either side
of it. On my pinkie finger, I noticed the small gold and diamond
bumblebee that I have been wearing for more than ten years.
And on that wrist I saw the gold bracelet my son made for me
one Mother's Day. On my right hand was a gold and diamond
bumblebee mounted on a wide gold band. This ring was a birthday present from my three children. All this jewelry is precious
sentimentally as well as financially. And all of it has withstood
time, remaining beautiful and sturdy. Just like joy, right, Jesus?

My eyes journeyed up my right arm to the scars resulting
from the second- and third-degree burns I received when I
dropped a deep fryer filled with boiling cooking oil one Fourth

of July as I was frying fish for our family celebration. I don't fully recall the excruciating pain, but the scars remind me of the event. When I burned my arm, the jewelry I was wearing, even though saturated in hot oil, was just as valuable after the experience as before. Just like joy that comes through our fiery trials, right, Jesus?

I focused again on the tub water and I thought, *How often do I put my hands in water? Maybe twenty times a day? And I put my hands in all kinds of water because I travel so much. I don't know about the chemicals in that water, whether it be hard or soft, fluorinated or not.* Yet the water has not, in any way, destroyed my jewelry. Because the gold and diamonds are real, not counterfeit. Just like Jesus' joy.

A few years ago thieves broke into our home and stole some of my jewelry. Thank God, we recovered a great deal of it. When we got it back, the quality of the jewelry was the same as before. But, like many women, I have bags of costume jewelry—three dresser drawers full, in fact. These bags contain little of monetary value; I just like the stuff. I can imagine that, if the thieves had grabbed some of that jewelry, they would have wanted to come back and toss the stuff in my face. The faux jewelry is counterfeit. It looks pretty for a while, but then it begins to fade, peel, and break. If you wear it in water long enough, it will turn your skin green. Of course, it would never make it through the hot oil.

Genuine versus counterfeit. Real versus fake. Long-lasting versus short-term. Joy versus happiness. The world didn't give me joy, and the world can't take it away. Joy gives me calm assurance even though I go through the valley of the shadow of death. Joy enables me to hold my peace when people say and do ugly things to me. When we go through troubles, afflictions, persecution, danger, illness, and distress, when the enemy comes to steal, kill, and destroy, we can have genuine joy in our hearts.

But one thing makes my jewelry very different from joy. The first time I was given a piece of fine jewelry, I was so excited I told my friends and a few of my enemies. I wanted everybody to know. But after I wore that jewelry for a short time, the thrill wore off, never to be regained.

Joy, on the other hand, is permanent. Once you have it, you never lose it. It may be overshadowed by human frailties, but real joy lasts for eternity.

"Father, I love our intimate conversations. You use symbols that we can identify with that help us understand you better. Draw to yourself those who haven't experienced your unspeakable, everlasting, abiding joy. Amen."

My Boat Is Sinking
Sheila Walsh

Our mouths were filled with laughter, our tongues with
songs of joy. Then it was said among the nations, "The
LORD has done great things for them."

PSALM 126:2

Laughter will get you through many a tough situation that
otherwise would sink your ship. For my husband, Barry, and
me, our dream boat sprung a leak when we were still at the airport. The writing was on the wall in letters sixteen feet high,
but we had on our holiday shades, and nothing was going to
dampen our spirits. We were off to the love boat! Well, not quite.

Sandi Patty, Max Lucado, Susan Ashton, and I were host-
ing a cruise from Boston to Bermuda. Barry and I were so
excited. We had never taken a honeymoon, and this was going
to be it. We were to be met at the airport by a limousine and
taken to the dock. During my growing-up years in Scotland, we
didn't even own a car. Now thoughts of all those years standing at bus stops were overprinted with images of being picked
up in a big, fat, shiny limo. Bliss!

No one was at the gate to greet us; so we assumed the driver would be waiting at baggage claim. "They won't want us to
carry our bags," I said to Barry.

We reached baggage claim and scoured the scene for a
sharply dressed, uniformed man holding a sign saying, "Barry
and Sheila, your carriage awaits." Twenty minutes later the baggage area was deserted except for Barry and me and our luggage.

"What do you think could have happened?" I asked my
equally bewildered husband.

"Stay here, and I'll call the cruise line," he said.

Ten minutes later he returned to report that they had forgotten about us and had suggested to him we should take a cab.

"I wish I had my camera handy," I said. "I'd love to snap a picture of us standing here in this deserted building. All dressed up and nowhere to go!"

We found a cab and were soon on our way to the dock.

"Which cruise line are you on?" the cab driver asked. We told him, but his only response was to say, "Ohh." I was beginning to suspect our love boat had started taking on major amounts of water.

The driver pulled up beside a lovely looking ship, and our spirits picked up.

"This looks great!" I said to Barry. "But why are all those people getting off the boat?"

"That's the crew," the driver said. "Two-thirds of them resigned this morning."

We climbed out of the cab and asked a man in uniform where we should put our bags to be taken on board. "If you ever want to see them again, I recommend you carry them yourselves," he replied.

I still have vivid memories of our struggling up the gangplank dragging our cases. When we reached the top, looking like refugees from a storm, one of the few people from the ship who hadn't resigned took our picture with a parrot.

Then we saw our cabin. I had imagined a lovely, spacious room with a view of the crystal clear waters below, fresh flowers in a vase, and music playing gently in the background. But when we opened the door, we both just stood there for a moment, stunned.

Then I lost it. I laughed so hard I fell over our bags. I wouldn't say the room was small, but we needed to take off our coats to get in. My pantry at home is bigger. We both laughed till tears ran down our cheeks.

"Let's go up on deck and get something to eat," Barry said. "You know what they say about all the great food on a cruise!"

When we arrived on deck, freezing rain greeted us, as did a line going all the way around the ship. "What's the line for?" I asked the person who had just joined it.

"Lunch," he grunted.

We were in that line for two hours and five minutes. All that was left of the lunch staff was one poor man who served cold pizza to twelve hundred people.

"Never mind," Barry said, as we both tried to squeeze into our cabin later. "We sail for Bermuda in ten minutes."

"This is your captain speaking," the voice over the intercom said. "I have some bad news. There is a hurricane at sea so we can't leave Boston harbor. Have a nice day."

You have to laugh! Laughter is a gift that will get you through the worst of times. Each of us can choose to lose it when life doesn't live up to our expectations, or we can let it go and laugh at the funny side of it all. Perhaps those who watch our jovial spirits will say, "Their God must be good."

"Lord, thank you for laughter. Help me to see the hilarity of it all and to share it today. Amen."

Sweet, Wise, and Spiritual
Luci Swindoll

✗♥✗♥✗♥✗♥✗♥✗♥✗♥✗♥✗♥✗♥✗♥
We shall be like him, for we shall see him as he is.

1 JOHN 3:2

O kay, let's get this over with: I'm not exactly a dog lover. I can count on one hand the dogs I really like—and have fingers left over!

You wonder why? I didn't grow up in a family that *had* to have a dog. Instead, my older brother Orville raised dogs for a short period of time, and we were all subjected to his inordinate dedication to the task. That's probably what did us all in. One litter of barking dogs in your backyard suffices to make you think you've done enough for the dog world.

Also, I find it difficult to own something that has to be fed constantly. As a single, on-the-go professional, I've never had cats, goldfish, hamsters, babies, or birds. My only pets are plants. I don't mind offering food and water to any living thing on occasion, but *every* day?

However, recently I met a dog I liked. I was in New York, sitting with my friend Mary in a little coffee shop on Columbus Avenue, when in walked a rather slovenly woman with her dog. Mary, noting a striking resemblance between this dog and hers, began a conversation.

"What's your dog's name? He's so cute."

I looked up from my newspaper in an effort to appear Christian and friendly. I'll admit, I was a *bit* curious.

"His name's Ben," the woman said warmly.

The dog never moved an inch from his owner. He kept his gaze riveted on her. When she shifted, he shifted. When she waited, he waited. Perfectly behaved and still, he stood there as though transfixed until it was time to move forward in the line. He followed, close at heel. The woman paid for her coffee and muffin, then she and Ben turned to leave. As they neared our table on their way out, Mary and the New Yorker continued to visit.

Mary said, "He's so well-behaved."

The woman assured Mary he had been very well-trained, was always attentive to her, and obedient to every command. With a loving expression, she then reached down, petted Ben, and said to us, "Yes, Ben is sweet, wise, and spiritual."

With that, the woman and dog exited the café. Mary and I looked at each other, exchanged big smiles, and pondered the thought. "Spiritual?"

Remembering the incident later, I realized how wonderful it would be if my Master described me that way. Sweet, wise, and spiritual. You know, that's exactly what we become when we spend enough time with him. Those qualities, which are his, are reflected in us. The more faithful we are to him, the more attentive to his voice, the more obedient to his way, the more we become the kind of person we want to be. The kind of person he created us to be.

I like Ben. He's a good reminder of the value of keeping one's eyes on the Master. If I want to be sweeter, wiser, and even more spiritual, I need to spend time with the One who longs to lead me through this life. The One who wants to take me out in public and have others see the true quality of his life in me.

"Lord, I desire to be more like you in every way. I know I can't begin to change in my own strength, so enable me by the power of your Spirit to reflect the sweetness and wisdom that come from spending time with you. May I value that more than anything. Amen."

Undergirded

For the Overtired, Overloaded, and Overwhelmed

❤✗❤✗❤✗❤✗❤✗❤✗❤✗❤✗❤✗❤✗❤✗❤

Flighty
Patsy Clairmont

✗♥✗♥✗♥✗♥✗♥✗♥✗♥✗♥✗♥✗♥✗♥

Flowers appear on the earth; the season of singing has
come, the cooing of doves is heard in our land.

SONG OF SONGS 2:12

Vou've heard of right-brained and left-brained. Well, I'm
bird-brained. No, not in regard to my cranial capacity but
referring to my love for winged creatures. A portion of my brain
takes great delight in the flight and fancy of birds.

I don't love all birds equally. For instance, I'm not terribly
fond of vultures or dodo birds. Now the gooney bird, he's pretty
entertaining, and the turkey, though not exactly handsome,
does trigger some succulent memories of holiday fare.

Even though I'm a bird-brained gal, I don't own any—birds
that is. Unless we were to count the darting hummingbirds who
entertain Les and me daily with their aerial bouts outside our
home. Like shimmering, streaked commas they hover over blos-
soms, sipping sweet nectar. Or the black-capped chickadees who
show up in their dapper attire and sing among the apple blos-
soms. And the cardinals flash their red brilliance as they dart
between the blue spruce. I'd like to think they are all mine. I
mean, I do feed them and at times clean up after them. Hmm,
sorta like family.

My all-time favorite feathered friend would have to be the
bluebird. Perhaps because seeing one is such an occasional happening it's a thrill when suddenly this blue wonder crosses your
path. Besides, if you ever see the sunlight refract off their feathers, your heart will take flight. The blue in bluebird takes on

new meaning as you memorize their unduplicated color. Amidst this sea of blue feathers is a blush of orange on their breast.

Bluebirds love open fields and fence posts. They aren't seed eaters; so to draw them into country yards takes birdhouses (mounted on fence posts) and birdbaths. We erected those items with wonderful success when we lived outside of town. Since we're once again city slickers, we no longer have the delight of daily visits. Now I have to be satisfied with glass bluebirds in my windowsills and antique bluebird dishes. But when I close my eyes and reminisce, I can still see them luxuriating in our birdbath, pleasing me beyond measure.

Have you noticed the mention of birds in the Scriptures? The Psalms say, "How lovely are Thy dwelling places, O LORD of hosts! The bird also has found a house, and the swallow a nest for herself, where she may lay her young" (Psalm 84:1, 3 NASB).

I choose to believe the "bird" is referring to a bluebird. Besides, the swallows and the bluebirds, even though they compete with each other for housing, are usually in nesting proximity. In this verse both birds have found lovely dwelling places. I like that. In fact, it mentions the birds even nest on the Lord's altars and how blessed are those who dwell in the house of the Lord. Hmm, even the birds can be examples.

David prayed for "the wings of a dove" that he might fly far away from his problems and be at rest (Psalm 55:6). I can get into that, can't you? At times I just want a fast, easy way out. I want to make my way to a hammock strung between two oaks at the water's edge where choirs of songbirds sing me to sleep.

Matthew tells us, "Look at the birds of the air; they do not sow or reap or store away in barns, and yet your heavenly Father feeds them. Are you not much more valuable than they?" (Matthew 6:26). Our heavenly Father provides for the birds. What a lovely thought; he, too, is a bird-watcher. And to think his care and provision for us is even greater, for he is a people-watcher, too. How comforting.

"*Father, thank you that you use all you have created to speak to us of your love . . . even the birds. Amen.*"

Pressing On—and We Ain't Talkin' Ironing

Thelma Wells

✖❤✖❤✖❤✖❤✖❤✖❤✖❤✖❤✖❤✖❤✖❤

Not that I have already obtained all this, or have already
been made perfect, but I press on to take hold of that for
which Christ Jesus took hold of me.

PHILIPPIANS 3:12

*E*very time we pick up a newspaper or turn on the news,
we receive a plethora of bad news. The government's state
of affairs isn't good. Shootings and murder, abuse and aban-
donment continue. Storms lash various parts of the country.
Eating certain foods causes disease; not eating others makes
us susceptible.

Sometimes I take a break from the world of news. My husband
taunts me, saying, "It's a shame a woman of your intelligence can't
talk intelligently about current affairs." Well, sometimes I choose
to be ignorant.

A woman in the Bible was plagued with bad news, but she
decided that rather than tuning out, she would press on. This
woman's name was never given to us, but we do know she had
a lot of problems. She had been sick with an issue of blood for
twelve years. Apparently, this woman, whom I've named Auntie Arlene because I feel kinship with her sufferings, had been
wealthy at one time. But she had spent all her money trying
to get well—and hadn't seen any progress. If bankruptcy had
been an option in her day, she could have qualified. Her relationships were disbanded because of her defiled physical condition, and her disease was progressing.

I admire this woman for two reasons. First, when she heard Jesus was coming to her town, she was determined to see him. She believed that, if she could just touch his clothes, she would be healed. Second, this woman never gave up hope despite her years of anguish and disappointment. Her faith was bigger than a mustard seed. She believed Jesus would remove the mountain of desperation and desolation from her life.

As Jesus entered the town, a large crowd immediately gathered around him. Picture a bunch of ants discovering a picnic. They excitedly swarmed around him, pressing in as tightly as possible.

I can imagine all kinds of people milling about him, with a variety of motives for doing so. Some were curiosity seekers, others wanted to catch him breaking the Jewish customs, some were members of the council of the High Court, still others were criminals looking for pockets to pick, a number were people who believed Jesus was the Son of God. And you could also toss in an assortment of Pharisees, Sadducees, tax collectors, women, children, disciples, and those who are always eager to see the latest miracle being performed.

Among this eclectic group was a synagogue ruler, Jairus, who pleaded with Jesus to heal Jairus's dying daughter. Jesus started off on his emergency run to Jairus's home when Auntie Arlene pressed her way through the crushing crowd to touch Jesus' cloak. Immediately her bleeding stopped, and she realized she was freed from her suffering.

Jesus, realizing power had gone out from him, turned around in the crowd and asked, "Who touched my clothes?" Right. It was like someone noting he was brushed against while standing in a ten-person elevator containing thirty squished people.

But Jesus visually searched through the mishmash of the crowd, looking for who touched him. The woman fearfully pressed through the crowd, fell at his feet, and told him the whole truth. That would be like giving your doctor a report on your condition in front of a crowd—humiliating, scary, yet wonderful. Imagine her relief when Jesus replied, "Daughter, your faith has healed you. Go in peace and be freed from your suffering" (Mark 5:34).

Auntie Arlene had pressed on until she reached the source of her healing. She believed Jesus could help her. And she had faith and determination that nobody or nothing was going to stop her from getting what she needed from Jesus.

Because we live in a fallen world, we will experience negatives in our lives. Heartache and disappointment will come our way. We experience "stuff" we don't deserve, don't want, and can't send back. It's ours. But thanks be to God, nothing happens in this world that he doesn't know about and that he can't handle.

Auntie Arlene's story shows that, regardless of the hurts you experience in life, you know someone who has the power to take those negatives and turn them into positives. You know someone whose holy powers aren't hindered by the crowd, by anyone's hidden agenda, by fear, by doubt, by whining, by complaining, or by other people's opinions. Nothing can negate Jesus Christ's power to bring healing and peace.

Each time we encounter a trial, wouldn't it be a relief if we could concentrate on Jesus' ability to handle it, if we could keep pressing on until we regained peace—just like Auntie Arlene? Despite everything she had been through, she managed to keep hope alive.

Someone once told me, "Don't get your hopes up. All that does is set you up for a letdown." I disagree. If I don't keep my hopes up, where will they go? Romans 5:3–5 says, "Not only so, but we also rejoice in our sufferings, because we know that suffering produces perseverance; perseverance, character; and character, hope. And hope does not disappoint us, because God has poured out his love into our hearts by the Holy Spirit, whom he has given us."

"Oh, Lord, how awesome you are. Just one touch of your garment can make the most defiled clean. You know all about what we encounter every day. You know the negatives that surround us at home, work, school, church, in the community, and in our minds. Please remind us that if we continue to press toward you without giving up, you will surely heal and deliver us from our anguish. Help us to encourage others to lean on you when they seem discouraged by this world's troubles. Let us be an example by seeking comfort and peace in Jesus' presence. For in his presence is joy beyond measure. Amen."

Is Anyone Awake?

Sheila Walsh

❌❤❌❤❌❤❌❤❌❤❌❤❌❤❌❤❌❤❌❤

Behold, I am coming soon! My reward is with me, and I
will give to everyone according to what he has done.

REVELATION 22:12

Well, I'm glad that God's awake!" my sister Frances said
as I finished telling her about the tornadoes that
touched down in Nashville the previous weekend and which
had blown themselves into my life but left me unscathed.

"Now let me tell you about my weekend," Frances said.

With the receiver cradled against my ear, I put on the teaket-
tle as I listened. I just knew that this was going to be a good story.

"I volunteered through the church to sing at the local nursing home this past Sunday," she began. "I knew it wasn't exactly
Carnegie Hall, but I wanted to bring a little joy to the senior
residents who don't get out much."

"How many were there?" I asked innocently.

"Physically there or mentally there?" she replied with a smile
in her voice.

"Just count the warm bodies," I said.

"Well, six people showed up. Three ladies fell asleep before
I started. Another was off in a corner dancing to a tune that
was different from the one I was singing, but the loudest one
of all sat right up front, just under my nose. She was so close
to me every time she sneezed I got a bath. Her hearing aid was
turned up too high, and it was giving off high-pitched whining noises that would have driven a dog mad. One of the nurses
tried to get her to back off a little, but the woman just yelled
at the nurse and told her to shut up."

. "Well, at least you had one enthusiastic listener," I suggested lamely.

"Not quite," Frances replied. "Every time I began another song she cried out at the top of her lungs, 'Oh, no, she's going to sing again!'"

We laughed for a while thinking about Frances's less-than-captivated audience.

"But, you know, Frances," I said, "what you said is right. God was awake. He didn't miss a single note."

Easy for me to say? Perhaps. But it's still true.

Do you ever feel as if you are killing yourself serving your children and your husband or your church or your friends, but no one seems to notice or appreciate you? We are told in so many ways what success looks like, what the woman of the nineties can do. Even in our churches we see those with high-profile ministries as the ones God is using.

I believe we need to resist that type of thinking. It's so discouraging—and it's so untrue. God sees our hearts, and that's all he cares about. He doesn't miss a single moment of a life lived out for him, whether it's in a spotlight or in a nursing home. That's why Frances will be back next Sunday being showered afresh by Bertha in the front row. Frances understands that even if Martha, Millie, and Mary are fast asleep, God is awake.

If everyone in your audience has dozed off or danced off to another tune, you might want to check again. There, in the corner, is God, watching and listening and appreciating you.

"Lord, thank you for my life. Thank you that every day is a gift from you. Thank you that I can offer every moment to you, and you gather them all up. Today I give you all the great and small moments, and I live them for you. In Jesus' name. Amen."

Join the Joy Squad
Barbara Johnson

Even youths grow tired and weary, and young men stumble
and fall; but those who hope in the LORD will renew their
strength. They will soar on wings like eagles; they will run
and not grow weary, they will walk and not be faint.

ISAIAH 40:30–31

My hair isn't gray, but my belt has had to cut me a little slack the last few years. As each birthday party comes, I try to be cool. But when my husband, Bill, lit the candles on my last Big-0 celebration, the young people started to sing "Kumbaya." (They thought it was a bonfire!) Then, when I noticed recently that one of the throw pillows on my bed was a hot water bottle, I had to admit maybe I am ... well, *maturing*.

God's Word says being tired, regardless of our age, isn't an issue if we wait on him. I've been waiting on the Lord a good many years and have discovered that wherever he is, joy is happening. I'll never be too old for that.

Isaiah 40 tells us soaring like an eagle through the currents of life is God's flight plan for us. We start out the trip by waiting on him. We learn to trust. Then we spread our wings and flap them. The result? We rise up and fall down, rise and fall, as we ride the currents. It looks effortless, and in many ways it is. The air currents themselves hold us up because we're relaxed and our wings are outstretched. Tighten up or fold up your wings, and you'll find yourself plummeting to earth—and an unfortunate landing.

Of course, were we not pushed into flight by our Father, we might never get beyond just waiting. God sets up circumstances that push us into trusting him to hold us up. It's the only way.

Mother eagles, I'm told, use that technique. They feather their nests with bits of jagged glass or splintered wood. When the wee ones hatch and grow, they are pricked by the sharp pieces and decide to take a flying leap out of the nest.

On that first dizzying flight, the young ones flap their wings like crazy as they try to find a current to slow their panic. With each trip, they learn when to ride the winds and when to dip, spin, or flap their wings. They learn how to rise above the worst, to soar higher and farther. Soon they're flying!

Growing up, growing wise, and growing in the Lord, we find we're not worn by trouble and experience but *renewed* through it. We understand that the eternal God is our refuge and "underneath are the everlasting arms" (Deuteronomy 33:27). Soon we're flying!

I believe in flying. In fact, I fly frequently all over the country. I put up with various inconveniences, flight delays, detours, turbulence, lost luggage, faraway rest rooms, missed connections, and bad food because the end result is worth the bother. I know I'm going to meet lovely, seeking, growing people who are eager to fly in the same direction as I am. Because I'm willing to fly, God places me in other people's lives, and he uses me to make someone smile, laugh, and look up. Then that person does the same for someone else, and that person will do the same for the next. Soon we're all soaring!

Have you ever watched the TV show, *Touched by an Angel?* The program reminds us that in each human body resides a living spirit looking for hope. People are in various levels of flight training. There are hurts and needs and loves. Many have fallen. All of us need to be touched, encouraged, challenged, or inspired. And we are meant to touch each other in some renewing way. We are all on assignment from God.

So I'm not ready to sit in a rocking chair, put up my feet, and stay put. I'm "plum" young in spirit, and I don't intend to end up like a prune. I dedicate myself to flying in God's Joy Squad. Want to sign up?

"Lord, thanks for coaxing us out of our safe nests into the world. Teach us to soar as we rest in you and to love others as we flit about, renewed by your strength every day. Amen."

Butcher, Baker, Candlestick Maker

Luci Swindoll

✖♥✖♥✖♥✖♥✖♥✖♥✖♥✖♥✖♥✖♥✖♥

Whatever your hand finds to do, do it with all your might,
for in the grave, where you are going, there is neither
working nor planning nor knowledge nor wisdom.

ECCLESIASTES 9:10

I'm not sure exactly when it hit me. I was running errands, pretty much going through the motions. Doing my routine. Suddenly I was finished and at home, and everything was out of the way. Easy as pie!

Then I stopped to think. First there was the bank to make a deposit. The teller could have done the work blindfolded; she was as fast as lightning. As always, I appreciated her help.

Next stop was the seamstress. I tried on ill-fitting clothes. With aplomb the alteration lady said, "No problem, we'll have these for you in ten days." *Great!* She's highly skilled in her craft, and I trust her implicitly.

Moving right along, I went to the service station where the mechanic replaced a fuse and serviced my car within the hour. I hardly know how to lift my automobile's hood, so I'm indebted to him for his experience and giftedness.

While that was being done, I dashed across the street to the hair salon for my appointment. My hair is a challenge for any hairdresser. I'm glad I have one who is well-trained and competent.

From there it was the doctor's office. We had a short consultation about my blood pressure, whereupon he changed the medication dosage. His expertise gives me enormous peace.

Off to the pharmacist who filled the prescription. I'm glad he's a professional!

Then I drove home. And I thought about the banker, the seamstress, the mechanic, the beautician, the doctor, and the pharmacist, who all serviced my needs in one morning and did it kindly. And quickly. For them, it was all in a day's work. For me, it was precisely what I needed to free me to do *my* work.

Work gets a tough rap sometimes, but it's really God's marvelous creation to engage us in meaningful ways and to make us productive. In his economy, to work is a gift. Work enables you to have purpose in life, cancel indebtedness, and be of genuine value to somebody else. Work is meant not just to occupy our time, but to engage our hearts. The apostle Paul says, "Whatever you do, work at it with all your heart, as working for the Lord, not for men, since you know that you will receive an inheritance from the Lord as a reward. It is the Lord Christ you are serving" (Colossians 3:23–24).

Work can be fun. Don't just drag off to work every day down in the mouth, thinking things are going to be awful. That can more often than not be a self-fulfilling prophecy. Life is basically what we make it. It starts in the mind and moves through the rest of the body. I determine every day to make my work enjoyable. I've always tried to do that. In so doing, I've learned new things and had a good time.

I appreciate people who put their heads down, best foot forward, shoulder to the wheel, nose to the grindstone, hand to the plow ... *and try to work in that position!*

All kidding aside, do your work as unto the Lord. And do it with gusto! What are you going to be when you grow up? Whatever it is, people like me will be deeply indebted to you for your service. When you go to work today, thank the Lord for the meaningful work you have and for your opportunity to help others. Give 'em a smile.

"I pray, Lord, you will create in me a spirit of joy and happiness in the work you have called me to do. Then, out of that joy, may I serve others kindly. Amen."

What a Pain
Patsy Clairmont

❌❤❌❤❌❤❌❤❌❤❌❤❌❤❌❤❌❤❌❤

Your rod and your staff, they comfort me.

PSALM 23:4

On a peppy morning, thinking myself more aerobic than I was or ever will be, I barreled down our second-floor stairwell and missed a step. My feet went skyward, and my tailbone came crashing down onto the exceedingly solid earth. Yikes! I hit a note so piercing neighborhood dogs had to be rushed in to the vet for treatment. Boy, did that smart. Well, smart might be too generous of a word for the situation.

Later I waddled back to the stairwell and counted the steps; they were all there. How I missed one I have no idea—although I have never been good at math. I did note, however, it was a long spell before I forgot that acrobatic equation. The touchy nature of the injury—or at least its tender location—meant every time I sat down it added up to pain.

Pain can be such a pain. I hate hurting; it's so draining. Besides, it can restrict our lifestyle, limit our activities, and dishearten us. It's hard to, say, play musical chairs with any enthusiasm when your tailbone is throbbing to the tune of *The Old Gray Mare*. Yet I have learned pain has purpose, which, at the peak of excruciating discomfort, brings me little consolation. Hindsight, though, has often proven pain's value. In fact, I have found pain to be one of life's most effective teachers. It gains one's full attention. It takes lessons down to the bottom (no pun intended) line (step).

A world without pain sounds great. But would it be?

My husband, Les, was returning from a restaurant-grocery store run. He had diet Pepsi in one hand and Chinese take-out in the other. His shoes were covered in snow as he stepped onto our tiled floor. That's where a calamity occurred that would change our lives. Les's feet went heavenward, and his body headed for that exceedingly solid earth. When his body landed, it was wedged between two walls. The angle and impact left his right ankle with four fractures.

Our son Marty and friend Dan helped me to escort Les to the emergency room. When the doctor asked Les what had happened, he told her I pushed him down the stairs while he was holding his six-pack. Thank you, Les. I assured her that I hadn't pushed him, there were no steps, and that the six-pack was pop. I was pleased to see his offbeat humor was still intact. But we were unaware of what this break meant for Les, or we might not have been chuckling. I did note the doctor's somber demeanor but wrote it off to one too many patients.

After Les spent months in a cast, we thought the tough part was over. But Les's diabetes added complications. When his cast was removed, we thought he was free to resume a walking lifestyle, which he did. His ankle was three times its normal size, but he had no pain. We continued on with life's daily demands. After a number of weeks, I noticed the side of his foot looked unnatural. We visited the doctor and found out that Les's ankle couldn't support his weight. It had begun to disintegrate, and the side of his foot, between his ankle and his heel, had caved in.

Les has been in a newfangled walking cast now for six months; the doctors are predicting he will have to wear it for years to come. At this stage he can only be on his feet ten minutes each hour. Life for us, in the time it took to slip, has changed.

Les didn't realize damage was occurring to his ankle because he had no pain. Had he felt the disintegration, he would have gone for medical counsel before such irreversible damage had occurred. Pain can save our lives both physically and spiritually.

Pain alerts us to problems. Pain assists in setting healthy boundaries. Pain can guide us into necessary changes.

The next time you feel pain—emotional or physical—remember that hurt can guide you to live more wisely and within the limits God has chosen to set for you individually. Ask him for insight into what adjustments you should make spiritually, physically, and emotionally to live within those limits. And then ask for the grace to do so.

"Dear Lord, we are comforted to realize you can use even pain for our benefit. Amen."

A Song in Her Heart
Thelma Wells

The LORD your God is with you, he is mighty to save. He
will take great delight in you, he will quiet you with his
love, he will rejoice over you with singing.

ZEPHANIAH 3:17

*O*ur family enjoys good gospel music. We have discovered
that praising God in song lifts our spirits, clears our heads,
and opens a place for the Holy Spirit to speak to us.

Alaya, my one-and-a-half-year-old granddaughter, is always
singing. From the moment she could utter sounds, she made
music. When her mother, Lesa, secured newborn Alaya in her
car seat, this child would make sounds. As she developed, those
sounds were easily recognizable as tunes such as the Barney
song, the ABC song, "Jesus Loves Me," "Row, Row, Row Your
Boat," and "Jesus Loves the Little Children."

Alaya sings when she is eating, having her diaper changed,
playing, standing, pulling up, watching television, bouncing in
her swing, sitting in a car, attending church. Everywhere, all
the time, she has a song in her heart.

At first I wondered how she kept the sweetness, calmness,
contentment, and joyfulness of singing all the time. But as I
thought about it, I decided Alaya has loving parents whom she
can depend on to take care of her, comfortable and safe surroundings to live in, little responsibility, a love of singing, lots
of attention when she sings, and joy because in her little heart
she feels God's love.

Just as Alaya feels secure and loved, God offers the same to
his children. He extends care to us by meeting our every need
(Philippians 4:19) and comforting us when we go through trials

(Psalm 23:4). He tells us to put our cares on him because he is responsible for our existence and future (1 Peter 5:6–7), stands ready to reveal to us truths about his Word (2 Timothy 2:15), and loves us so much he sacrificed his Son to save us from eternal damnation (John 3:16).

Realizing all this, don't you think we have something to sing about? When you're going through your daily routine or when you face trials and tribulations, do you allow music to comfort you? When times are good, do you stop to sing for joy?

God enjoys the song we lift up in praise to him. He even reciprocates by singing back to us, as the verse in Zephaniah tells us, "He will rejoice over you with singing."

Just think, when we sing praises down here on earth, angels are singing around God's throne twenty-four hours a day, seven days a week: "Holy, holy, holy, Lord God Almighty, the earth is full of your glory." And we'll be joining them. An old Negro spiritual says, "If you miss me from singing down here and you can't find me nowhere, come on up to bright glory. I'll be singing up there."

Want to lift your spirits from the hustle and bustle of the day? Sing to the Lord. When praises go up, blessings come down. Now, isn't that something to sing about?

"Master of music and all good things, I adore you. You create a melody of sweet singing in the hearts of those who love you. Even if we can't sing melodiously, we can sing for joy at the works of your hands. We can praise you in the morning, afternoon, evening, and the midnight hour. And you sing back to us. What a promise! Thank you that melodies linger on in our hearts long after our voices have given way. We appreciate that it's not the sound of our voices that moves you but the condition of our hearts. Amen."

Cast Those Cares Away

Barbara Johnson

✖♥✖♥✖♥✖♥✖♥✖♥✖♥✖♥✖♥✖♥✖♥

Cast all your anxiety on him because he cares for you.

1 PETER 5:7

I overheard two five-year-old girls talking. The first said, "I'm stressed out!"

The second said, "You can't be stressed out. That's only for grown-ups!"

Sure enough, the accent may be on youth these days, but the stress is on adults. Always reflecting on the things we haven't done, we start each day worrying earlier and stay up later to worry every night.

A certain parish priest patented a method for making holy water. I figure it's a good way to deal with worries, too. He took a big pot, filled it with water, turned up the heat, and boiled the devil out of it.

And guilt? Why not boil the devil out of that, too? After all, we'll always have those things we shouldn't have done but did anyway. So we end up wasting time dragging our burden of guilt in the dirt instead of getting it washed.

Some of us are learning that cares are the tools God uses to fashion us for better things. He uses reverses to move us forward. Reverses and cares bow us down low until we finally drop to our knees. But a lot of kneeling keeps us in good standing because it brings us closer to God. Being close to God, we find peace. Even if our cares aren't resolved as we wish and even if we finally have to admit life in this world will never be safe or predictable, we may discover that's because we were made for another place.

In the meantime, one way to handle your concerns is to select a handful, put them in a day-pack, and set out for a beautiful place near your home. Include a pencil and a notepad. When you find a shady spot, unpack those worries one at a time. Turn each one over in your mind and make notes about how it bothers you. What is it about each one that makes you not want to turn loose? Can you imagine your life without that particular worry? What would life feel like without it? What would it look like?

Decide which cares you can live without. Then toss them, one at a time, into a river, over the side of a cliff, or into a trash can. Watch them float or fall away. Think about how God formed us, sin deformed us, and Jesus transforms us. Your day-pack and your heart will be lighter on the way home.

If you live in a city and have no quiet spot in nature, go to the local party store and buy a helium balloon. Take it home and write out each of your worries on a separate piece of paper. Roll up the notes; then tie them to the end of the balloon's ribbon. Take it into your backyard and hold it up as high as you can. Stand on your tiptoes. Let the balloon go. Watch it sail away with your worries attached. You are letting heaven have them.

Don't be upset if later those same worries settle back on your front porch. Let them bring you to your knees again. Instead of shouting, "Panic! Stress! Chaos!" think, *Just another routine day full of opportunities to get close to God.* Smile. Go get another balloon.

If, even in worries, you stay next to God and his grace, you won't have to say much—it'll show on your face. Don't get stressed out, get blessed out!

"Jesus, you know I can't add a single hour to my life by worrying. So I'm giving up my cares—just for today. I will walk in your way one day at a time. I will let the stress lead me to you. Amen."

Giddy Gifts

Marilyn Meberg

✗♥✗♥✗♥✗♥✗♥✗♥✗♥✗♥✗♥✗♥♥

Every good and perfect gift is from above.

JAMES 1:17

I'm going to tell you a little secret about Patsy Clairmont. At this moment, only two people in the world know what it is. Naturally, after you've read this, we will have broadened the secret base considerably. You are expected to tell your friends so this information can be circulated widely. But before I drop the secret on you, let me give you some background.

When we six speakers do a Women of Faith conference, fruit, cheese, and cracker baskets are delivered to our rooms on Friday night after our first meeting. We're grateful for this little basket because we're usually hungry and feel the need of a snack before bed. Also, it provides an opportunity to unwind. Sometimes we gather in each other's rooms, nibble the basket's offerings, talk about the audience's response and people with whom we've visited at our book tables, and ruminate about how we're feeling.

This past weekend we were in Omaha, and Patsy's hotel room was down the hall from Pat's and mine. On Friday night she joined the two of us in the basket ritual by bringing her rather large Gouda cheese round with her, which she was gnawing when I opened the door for her to come in. The three of us sat around amiably gnawing our cheese rounds. For some reason no knives were in the baskets.

I soon had my fill of purple grapes, cheese, and crackers. Then I noted I hadn't heard Patsy's voice for a number of minutes. Looking over at her sitting cross-legged on my bed, I saw she was absorbed with a fragment of the red wax in which the

79

cheese had been encased. She was pressing it between her fingers and rolling it in the palms of her hands. She looked utterly contented.

"What in the world are you doing, Patsy?" I asked.

"Have you ever played with this red wax cheese covering?" she asked in such a quiet voice I could hardly hear what she said.

"Well, no, I never have."

"You should try it . . . it's very satisfying," she said as I stretched forward to catch her soft words.

Soon all three of us were pressing, rolling, and shaping little fragments of the wax encasement, and it was indeed satisfying. In fact, it brought back happy memories of plying Play-Doh with my children. I always loved it when they would agree to settle in for a good session of Play-Doh.

Fatigue soon replaced contentment as the three of us hunkered over our cheese wax, so we called it a night and went to bed. On Saturday morning, as one of the speakers was sharing her life with twelve thousand women in the arena, Patsy quietly dipped into her purse and pulled out a wax cheese wrapper fragment. Glancing slyly at me, she began to work the wax—rolling, squeezing, shaping, rolling again, reshaping . . .

After some time had passed, I leaned over to her and with teacher-like haughtiness whispered, "Don't you think you should be paying attention?"

Unperturbed, she whispered back, "I always concentrate better when I'm doing something else, too."

Later, when we were debriefing, it was obvious Patsy hadn't missed a word. That was a bit deflating for me because any one task requires my full attention or I end up in the weeds.

On our flight back to Palm Springs, Patsy was sitting in front of Pat and me. Shortly after takeoff, she wordlessly handed each of us yet another wax fragment she had gathered up from the bottom of her purse. We set about rolling, squeezing, and shaping until we skidded onto the runway of the Palm Springs airport.

Patsy and I were both attending a social event the next evening, and though I must admit I didn't have a good view of Patsy's left hand, I was almost certain she was serenely rolling a small piece of red wax between her fingers while carrying on a perfectly intelligent—even animated—conversation with several people. Surely that one cheese wax encasement had to have been used up by now. How did she manage to have an unending supply of little red wax fragments in her purse? Did she head out in the dead of night and buy huge rounds of cheese in order to have wax fragments for her purse? Frankly—and here's the secret—I'm pretty sure she has an addiction. Tsk, tsk, and to think it's red wax.

But I have to tell you another secret. I think I might be addicted, too. Several nights ago I found myself enjoying the six o'clock news far more than usual. I seemed more relaxed and not quite as troubled by the various atrocities I was seeing. Could it be because I was rolling a red wax fragment between my fingers?

This morning I was talking with Pat on the phone and said, "You're sounding pretty happy."

"Well, actually I am."

"What's the reason? I mean, you can't be happy without a reason," I badgered.

"Well," she said, "I was rummaging through my purse looking for my checkbook, and guess what I found?" I didn't need to ask any more questions; I knew.

I've said it before and I'll say it again: Some of life's greatest pleasures come from insignificant and unexpected things. When God says he has given us all things to enjoy, I don't think he's talking just about the grandeur of mountains, sunsets, and waterfalls. It's anything that gives us pleasure and is in accordance with his will.

I don't want to allow the demands of life to blind me to the little joys that pop up every day. Appreciating those little joys frequently provides the stamina for the big demands. God strengthens, and God enables; that truth is presented clearly in his Word. But I'm convinced he sends little perks along as part of his encouragement.

"Lord, may I not be too sophisticated, stuffy, or busy to miss the little things that can encourage me and give me pleasure. I thank you that you are the author of all good gifts—big or small. May I see them and receive them as evidence of your multidimensional love for me. Amen."

Are You Finished with That?

Sheila Walsh

❤✗❤✗❤✗❤✗❤✗❤✗❤✗❤✗❤✗❤✗❤✗❤

Do not be anxious about anything, but in everything, by
prayer and petition, with thanksgiving, present your
requests to God.

PHILIPPIANS 4:6

Do you experience times when there doesn't seem to be enough to go around? Bills are piling up faster than paychecks, and anxiety is creeping into your mind.

Many such moments have occurred for me, making me acutely aware that the bread on my plate came from the Lord because my cupboard was bare. When I was part of British Youth for Christ, I was paid a minimal salary. Usually I had just enough to keep me in hose and shampoo—and on my knees.

One of my memories from that time is of Phil, a staff evangelist, and his wife who splurged one night and went to a nice restaurant for a steak dinner. While they were enjoying a lovely meal, Phil noticed that the man seated opposite them was leaving after only picking at the T-bone steak.

"More than three-quarters of that steak is left," Phil said to his wife indignantly. "What a waste!"

"Never mind what he's doing," she replied. "Enjoy your meal."

"But that's a huge piece of steak, and it'll go to waste," Phil continued. "They'll throw it out."

A few minutes passed, and then he said, "I'm sorry, but I just can't allow that to happen."

As he stood up, his wife hissed at him, "Sit down! What are you going to do?"

"Never you mind," he whispered. With that he sneaked over to the table, wrapped the large piece of meat in his napkin, and then slipped back into his seat.

"What did you do that for?" she asked in disbelief. "What are you going to do with it?"

"I'll give it to the dog," he said.

Two minutes later, the man who had been sitting at the table returned from the rest room to an empty plate. He called the waiter over and demanded to know what had happened to his meal. The poor waiter didn't have a clue as to its whereabouts, but he did casually wonder why that nice young couple was leaving without finishing their meal.

God's provision is seldom on the plate at another table. When you find yourself looking at a bank balance that couldn't keep a goldfish afloat, remember who you are. Your Father knows every need before you even voice it. He knows every unexpected turn of events. We are told by Paul to be anxious about nothing. "Nothing" is a pretty conclusive word. No thing, no part, no portion.

Whatever is weighing you down, stop what you're doing (which I guess at the moment is reading!), and with thanksgiving on your lips, bring your requests to God. You won't have to eat what's on someone else's plate; God will give you your own.

"Thank you, Lord, that you care for me. Thank you that you see every need before I even voice it. Right now, with a grateful heart, I bring my concerns to you. Amen."

Turning Over a New Leaf

And Finding the Joy

×❤×❤×❤×❤×❤×❤×❤×❤×❤×❤×❤×❤×❤×❤

The Main Line

Thelma Wells

❤✖❤✖❤✖❤✖❤✖❤✖❤✖❤✖❤✖❤✖❤

This is the confidence we have in approaching God: that if
we ask anything according to his will, he hears us.

1 JOHN 5:14

*O*n a beautiful April day in Dallas, I was soaking in the
refreshing sun rays. The temperature was a comfortable
eighty degrees, and the breeze softly surrounded my shoulders
as if God were cradling me in his arms. Birds were chirping in
the background. Our front lawn was a splendid carpet of green,
topped by two magnificent, thirty-year-old magnolia trees. As
I looked up toward the heavens, not a cloud was in the sky.

But then something grabbed my attention. About forty feet
above the carpet of grass were lines of cable wires laced together
in conduits swagged from tall poles. The network of wire connected to other cables on other poles and to houses and more
poles and houses . . . I hadn't noticed all this circuitry before.

As I thought about it, I realized these masses of wires make
it possible for us to talk with our friends via telephone, e-mail,
fax, and telegraph. Because of these lines, we could have money
wired to my bank account. We could receive instant news about
peace treaties and the weather as it happens. We have access
to college studies and home decorating; cooking and remod-
eling; the symphony and the theater—all through these wires
that crisscross themselves from one pole to another.

But then I thought, *What happens when it storms, and these
cables are down? We can't call for help. We can't send a message
to anyone. We feel out of control and isolated. What we have taken
for granted is no longer a source of contact for us.*

An old Negro spiritual reminds us of the most important connection we can make.

Jesus is on the main line.
Tell him what you want.
Jesus is on the main line.
Tell him what you want.
Jesus is on the main line.
Tell him what you want.
Call him up and tell him what you want.

Have you ever attempted to get in touch with God and found yourself doubting his ability to help you? Do you find yourself worrying about things you should tell God about instead? Do you feel ashamed to talk to God? Do you find yourself seeking other people's opinions rather than relying on God's guidance? Do you think you have to use a certain posture or language to get God's attention? Do you think you've done something so awful you can't tell God?

If your answer is "yes" to any of those questions, you're creating unnecessary interference between you and God. Nothing can keep you from being directly connected to God if you want to be.

It doesn't matter what time of day or night it is; what day of the week it is; who else is talking to him; or what the problem is. He is always available to listen and to help us without static or interference. His omnipotence has blocked out anything and everything that would keep him from hearing and answering us.

When you need to make decisions and nobody on earth understands, call him up.

When your problems seem unbearable, call him up.

When you want to praise him and show appreciation for his wonderful work in your life, call him up.

When you want to communicate with someone who wants to communicate with you and who has all the answers to your questions, call him up.

It doesn't matter if the telephone lines are down all over the world, God is always available. The only interference that can hinder our communication is our rebellion and disobedience. Even then, he is ready and willing to forgive us and to accept our call. He's always near to comfort and cheer just when we need him most.

"God, sometimes I create interference when I'm trying to get to you. Maybe my faith is shaken or I have pouts or doubts. I don't try to contact you when I need direction because I try to do it myself. Sometimes I neglect togetherness with you because I'm lazy or just don't feel like it. What a consolation to know I'm the problem, not you. Thank you for always keeping your communication line open. Your listening ear is my source of comfort. Amen."

The Night Winter Ran Away
Sheila Walsh

✘♥✘♥✘♥✘♥✘♥✘♥✘♥✘♥✘♥✘♥✘♥

Carry each other's burdens, and in this way
you will fulfill the law of Christ.

GALATIANS 6:2

Have you noticed how much easier it is to carry someone else's burden rather than your own? When we take our eyes off our own needs and reach out to someone else, we often find our prayers were answered when we weren't looking. This principle reminds me of a story I made up for my little boy, Christian.

Long ago on a horse farm in the cold north of Canada lived a small boy whose name was Joe. He lived with his Uncle Tom, Aunt Sara, and cousin Michael.

Some nights when Joe couldn't sleep he would stand at his bedroom window and watch the horses in the field below. Their breath in the frozen air looked like steam trains racing through the night.

One horse always stood alone. He was white with just a touch of black on his nose as if he had been kissed by Santa Claus after he climbed down a sooty chimney on Christmas Eve.

Joe loved this horse. He felt the horse's unspoken sadness and shared it. When Joe was four years old, he lost his mother and father in a car accident as they hit a patch of ice on a winter's night. Now Joe lived with his mother's sister and her family. They loved him. They tucked him into bed each night with stories of bears and giants, bicycles and boys. But still, when all the lights in the house were dimmed, Joe would stand alone at the window and watch the white horse.

Joe began to talk to God about the white horse he had named Winter. He found it easier to talk about the horse than about himself. "Dear God, please help Winter," he prayed. "He seems so lonely and sad. Please bring him a friend."

When morning came and the first ribbon of sun would rest on his pillow, Joe would race to the window to see if his prayer had been answered. But the white horse still stood alone.

After a number of such mornings, Joe made up his mind he would be the one to help Winter, no matter what it took. After breakfast when Uncle Tom was working in the barn, Aunt Sara was busy with the laundry, and Michael had torn out of the house, late again for school, Joe crossed the field to put his plan into action.

"Hello, Winter," he said as he climbed up onto the fence that edged the field. "I'm going to help you find a family."

The white horse moved toward Joe and touched Joe's cheek with his own. They stood like that for a moment, and neither of them felt alone. "We'll leave tonight," Joe said. Winter nodded as if he understood.

That night Joe was surprised by the wind that whipped the fall leaves around his feet like dancers urging him to stay in the house as he stepped out into the cold. He made his way in the moonlight to the gate at the far end of the field. "Come on, boy," he called to the white horse.

For a moment Winter didn't move as if weighing the life he had come to know against what the night would hold for him and his little friend. Then he moved toward the gate and gently nuzzled Joe's neck. Joe was too small to saddle the horse so Joe stood on the gate and climbed onto Winter's back, clinging to his mane.

"Come on, boy," Joe said and urged the horse away from the farm. They walked for miles. Joe's eyes were tired and heavy. His hands were sore from holding onto Winter's mane. They walked on. Joe's eyes began to close. He tried to stay awake. He tried to hold onto the white horse, but sleep closed in on him. As his hands lost their hold, he fell from Winter's neck onto the cold ground.

Joe opened his eyes. The light hurt, and he closed them. He wondered where he was. He remembered the cold night and the wind. He opened his eyes again and saw Aunt Sara and Uncle Tom sitting on the edge of his bed. Aunt Sara had tears running down her cheeks.

"Winter!" Joe cried. "Where's Winter?"

"He's fine," Aunt Sara said through her tears. "He was standing over you like a guardian angel when we found you."

"First time I've ever seen him standing with anyone!" said Uncle Tom with a laugh.

"I tried to find his home," Joe said.

"Looks like his home is with you now, boy," Uncle Tom replied. "He wouldn't leave your side."

Sometimes when we forget ourselves and focus on the needs of another, God answers our deepest prayers.

"Lord, teach me to forget myself and love others. Amen."

Championship Play

Patsy Clairmont

The tongue of the wise makes knowledge acceptable.

PROVERBS 15:2 nasb

I would like to introduce you to my friend Maven, whom, by the way, I happen to hate. I know, I know, we shouldn't hate—and if we do, we surely shouldn't publish the fact. But Maven isn't exactly real, although he does have a consistent personality—aggravating. The reason I say he is my friend is because I have purposed to spend time in his company, and we converse regularly. Maven is a man of extensive vocabulary, and trust me, he has an immovable will.

You see, Maven is my computer Scrabble opponent. He came built into my favorite word game so I would always have someone to challenge, but he doesn't play fair. In fact, he often speaks a language I don't understand—and without apology. Our game-playing relationship has developed by degrees. We started out as novices and have made our way to championship bouts. I don't mind when Maven wins ... well, perhaps I do, but I wouldn't if he would communicate more clearly. C'mon, listen in and see what you think.

I scan my tiles and decide on the word *boast* to begin the game. Maven, who continually boasts, attaches to *boast* the word *teleosts*. Okay, troops, what is *teleosts*? I stop the game and look it up. It is a bony fish (and Maven is a bonehead).

Next I spell the word *brains*, which I'm obviously in need of. It connects to a double-word score. Things are looking up. My opponent puts down *eme*. *Eme? Eme?*

"Maven, you're pushing me." I look up *eme*, and I'm told it means "an uncle." Hmm, I'm beginning to suspect a conspiracy between Maven and the built-in Scrabble dictionary, which was probably written by Maven's Uncle Eme.

I then arrange my tiles to spell *elite*. So there, Mav.

He takes his turn and spells out *enure*. I look it up and am told it means "inure." Oh, that really clears things up. So I challenge *inure* and find out it means, "to accept something unacceptable."

"Maven, you're unacceptable!" I yell.

I toss down the word *pilot*. Maven adds to the board *ratton*. Yikes! This guy really gets on my nerves. So I head for the dictionary again. *Ratton* means "rat." Hmm, fitting.

I exchange five of my letters to improve my rack. Maven pauses. (Did I hear someone chortle?) Then he empties his entire rack to create the word *coopting*, with the "g" landing on the triple-word score. *Coopting*, I discover, means to "elect," and so I elect to quit!

A graphic in the electronic Scrabble game as you depart the system depicts the game board being thrown down and shattering into a gazillion pieces. I like that a lot. It feels extremely satisfying; almost as if I got in the last word.

Words can open our understanding, but words can also bring us into conflict with others. At times it's as if our opponents (husband, child, friend, stranger) have been speaking an unknown language. For we haven't understood them nor have they had a clue as to what we were trying to convey.

We need to take the time to search out each other's meanings and not treat our relationships like a game in which we rack up points. Let's not quit trying, let's not throw in the towel, and let's not walk away angry (although cool-down breaks can be helpful). Perhaps then we can hear beyond the words to the language of the heart.

"You, Lord, are our champion. Teach us to value people even more than the tantalizing last word. May we lean in and truly hear each other. Amen."

Storm Warning

Marilyn Meberg

To all who received him, to those who believed in his
name, he gave the right to become children of God.

JOHN 1:12

Vacate your room immediately and head for the stairwell.
Proceed to the main ballroom on the first floor. This is not
a drill ... vacate your room immediately." Those of us who travel
together for the Women of Faith conferences had been in our
Nashville hotel rooms for only fifteen minutes when this fre-
netic voice came crackling over the intercom.

Prior to this message, I was looking out my twenty-fourth-
story window, commenting that the sky had become ominously
dark. Peering over my shoulder, Mary Graham had noted lightning dancing crookedly down the street below us. Luci, ever
the shutterbug, had shouted, "I have to get my camera. This
is amazing!" Instinctively, we all had drawn back from the window as we became aware of the building's swaying motion.

"Good grief," I had said intelligently. "Is this a tornado? I've
never been in a tornado. Scores of earthquakes, but never a tornado!" No one was interested.

My storm suspicions were then confirmed not only by the
voice on the intercom but also by the debris flying past the window. When a portion of the metal facade from the front of the
hotel went hurtling by, we decided to hotfoot it to the stairwell. As we staggered by Luci's room (the motion had reduced
us to unseaworthy sailors), Luci was faced with the dilemma
of blowing away for the sake of a memorable photo or joining
us in the stairwell. Deciding on the stairwell, we all began the
trek down twenty-four flights.

"Mercy, is this only the fourteenth floor?" I gasped as everyone went huffing past me—everyone except Luci. We decided we weren't interested in making it to the ballroom anyway. As far as I was concerned, sitting cross-legged in the corner of the stairwell had become increasingly attractive. Luci thought anything was more attractive than hiking down ten more flights; so she voted for joining me in the corner. The lady in front of me from New Jersey liked the idea, too. The problem was that there really wasn't a corner; if we just sat down, we would be an obstruction to those determined to reach the ballroom. Reluctantly, the lady from New Jersey, Luci, and I rejoined the heavy breathing procession and headed on down.

The odd thing was I didn't think we needed to be doing this. The building wasn't moving anymore. I heard no storm sounds and was sure whatever little thing had happened was over with.

When we finally reached the first floor, I was stunned to see smashed cars on the streets, and broken glass, pieces of roofing, and unidentifiable stuff littering the pavement. The glass-covered gazebo that domed the hotel bar was shattered; insulation fragments and dust covered everything. Threading our way through the broken glass, we were hustled into the ballroom with the warning that another tornado was due to touch down in a matter of moments. Several people were lying on the floor being fanned by friends, and one woman, who had a heart attack, was later taken out by ambulance.

Well, Marilyn, so much for your assumption this wasn't a big deal, I thought sheepishly.

Three hours later, the storms had passed, and we were allowed to leave the ballroom. Fortunately, our hotel was pronounced structurally safe, the elevators were put back in operation, and we resumed our lives.

Later, as we watched the local television news and saw the horrific devastation resulting from the tornadoes, we realized how serious the storms had been. We also saw how fortunate we were in being spared greater destruction.

That night, lying in my bed listening for wind and wondering if the room were swaying again, I realized a salvation message was tucked into the experience. When I had been staring out the window and then told to vacate the room, what if I had chosen not to? As it turned out, I would have survived.

But what if I had said, "Yes, I know there's a tornado out there. I can even see it. But I'm going to stay here anyway." It wasn't enough for me just to believe the tornado was raging through Nashville; I had to do something about what I believed.

Haven't you known people who have said, "Of course I believe in Jesus. I believe he is the Son of God." But they didn't act on that belief; they just stood at the window seeing all the evidence but doing nothing about it. To become a child of God, I must believe Jesus is the Son of God. Then I must respond by receiving Jesus as Savior, accepting forgiveness of my confessed sin, and believing he has entered into my interior being where he will stay with me through all the storms of my life.

As I was ruminating on these thoughts, Pat leaned over, turned on the light, and said, "Are you all right, Marilyn? You're whispering."

"Sure, I'm fine. I was just doing a bit of sermonizing I guess."

"Really ... about what?"

"Acting on what you believe ... not being passive about it."

Studying the wall for a minute she asked, "Do you think the building is swaying?"

"I don't believe so, but if I did, I'd act on it!"

"Lord, thank you that you invite me to participate in becoming a member of your family. Help me never to lose sight of the importance of my believing and receiving. Enable me also to believe and receive the blessings you want to give me. I don't want to stand at the window and simply observe; I want to partake in a rich relationship with you. Amen."

A Heart-y Ha, Ha, Ha!

Barbara Johnson

✗♥✗♥✗♥✗♥✗♥✗♥✗♥✗♥✗♥✗♥

A cheerful heart is good medicine, but a crushed spirit
dries up the bones.

PROVERBS 17:22

They say three kinds of people populate the world: Those who can count and those who can't. As you can see, I'm in the latter category. As I always say, give me ambiguity or give me something else. And I've always wondered why *abbreviation* is such a long word.

Despite my math deficiency, uncertainty, and puzzlement, there's one problem I don't have. I'm not like certain pious Christians who suffer from the haunting fear that someone, somewhere, may be happy. I'm out to be a joy germ!

We have to be on the lookout for fun, whether it be in simple things like funny signs ("Our fish are so fresh you want to smack 'em!"); funny names (if Fanny Brice had married Vic Tanny, her name would have been Fanny Tanny); or funny bumper stickers ("Forget about World Peace. Visualize using your turn signal.").

Just today I called my friend, Mary Lou, who at one time in her struggles was so far out you couldn't even find her with radar. But she has a marvelous sense of humor, and we have laughed and cried together many times. I've learned a lot from her about coping. But today she caught me off guard. She told me that, when she really feels down, she has a special way of lifting her spirits. I waited for her to explain, expecting some spiritual gem to fall from her lips. Instead, she told me, "I get out an old Shirley Temple video and a box of chocolate chip cookies and lie down for a couple of hours to escape."

Maybe some time with Shirley will perk you up, too. You might want to substitute Ry-Krisps for the cookies so you don't have to roll in the door when you reenter reality. Of course, some people say reality is a crutch for those who can't handle drugs.

But, according to my calculations, reality is this very second. You see, yesterday is only a memory, and tomorrow is merely a dream. Today is an illusion. That leaves this one second. Every day you have 86,400 seconds. But they come only one at a time. In your bank account of time, no balance is carried over until the next day. You use those seconds or lose them. There is no chance to reinvest.

Make your investment wisely by believing you deserve to be full of joy this very second. And you can be. Decide to be.

Find out what brings you joy. Have fun in a myriad of ways. Don't put it off until you finish your chores; instead, make tedious tasks a game. Compete with yourself. Reward yourself. Make work, play.

Be curious about everything and everyone. You'll get tickled in the process!

Trust the heavenly Father of goodness. Giggle at his artistic genius in the world. Always remember you're created unique—just like everyone else!

I tell you, I'm not going to fret just because a neighbor is a few fries short of a Happy Meal, or another driver on the California freeway doesn't have all his corn flakes in one box. So what if my chimney's clogged and my husband's belt doesn't go through all the loops? As a born-again believer, I have accepted God's forgiveness in the salvation of Jesus Christ, and I can freely forgive others and joyfully move on. Learning all I can from my mistakes, I better tolerate the mistakes of others. If there is a problem I can't change, with the Lord's help, I turn it into something beautiful.

Yes, joy is free, but it doesn't come cheaply. It's based on who I am, not what I have, where I'm headed, or where I've been. It's a biblical choice, and it's the best option—every single second of the day!

"Dear God, you give the oil of joy for mourning and the garment of praise for the spirit of heaviness. You are my 'life savor' today and in every situation. Help me to enjoy the seconds given to me today. Every last one of them! Amen."

Mothers I Have Known

Luci Swindoll

But we were gentle among you, like a mother
caring for her little children.

1 Thessalonians 2:7

Beth is the most wonderful mother. Granted, her children are still babies, but she is off to a great start. She has finished a master's program in psychology, traveled in Europe, worked in a drug rehabilitation clinic, and lived an adventuresome life. Yet, her real colors shine when she is with her two boys. She was *made* for motherhood. And why not?

You see, I know her mother, Marilyn, with whom I've been friends since Beth was five. I've watched as Marilyn gave Beth love, affection, discipline, a fun childhood, and wise mentoring. Marilyn encouraged Beth to be her best, introduced her to Jesus Christ at a young age, cheered her growth and development as an individual, and helped to provide her a good education. Marilyn was a caring, strong, unique mother, and one I admired greatly. But why wouldn't she be?

You see, I knew *her* mother, Elizabeth. Beth's grandmother was one of the most interesting women I've ever known. Quiet and reserved, she had a ready wit and smile. A wonderful listener, she was always eager to spend time with her daughter and her grandchildren, listening to their joys or woes. Her love of reading and learning was passed down to the next generation, then the next. Elizabeth established a pattern for mothering that Marilyn emulated, and now, Beth.

As a single person with no children, let me say I believe life's highest calling is motherhood. An endeavor like no other, it demands a sense of selflessness that must be renewed every day.

I enjoy watching my friends interact with their children. It's fascinating. Just the other day Sheila said being a mother is the great leveler of humanity. (She has an adorable baby boy.)

"On Monday morning, Christian doesn't care that I'm tired from speaking all weekend," she explained. "He wants to go to his swimming lesson and wants me to take him. So I get up and go. It's as simple as that." (I guess he doesn't know she's Sheila Walsh!)

An article appeared in the *LA Times* recently about the California Mother of the Year.* Her name is Barbara Hoche. She has three daughters. Wanting to be actively involved in their lives, she was their room mother, a PTA officer, a Brownie troop leader, and a Sunday school teacher. She escorted the girls to movies and plays and took them shopping.

Mothers engage in these activities all the time, but Barbara Hoche is remarkable because she is confined to a wheelchair. Mrs. Hoche was hit by an automobile as a twenty-year-old student and was paralyzed. Now she's seventy-one.

The article was filled with high praise from her daughters: "When we were little, Mother would lay us across her lap and off she'd go through the house." Or, "When we were older, she'd take us shopping, and if we got tired, we'd sit on her footrests and she'd scoot across the mall."

Fluent in Bulgarian, she served as a translator in the 1984 Olympics. Her thirty-six-year-old daughter said, "I got comments all the time from friends saying they wished they had a mother like mine."

You may not be a mother, but you have a mother. Did you know the only one of the Ten Commandments that carries a promise with it is the one about honoring your parents? "Honor your father and your mother, so that you may live long in the land the LORD your God is giving you" (Exodus 20:12). God blesses with

---

*"Celebrating Being Alive," *Los Angeles Times*, March 30, 1998.

longevity those who hold their mothers in high regard. Call your mother today and say, "I love you. I'm glad you're my mom."

Those were the last words I said to my mother on the night she died suddenly at the age of sixty-three. The day I'm writing this devotional is her birthday. She would have been ninety-one. I'm glad I called.

"*Heavenly Father, with tremendous gratitude I thank you for mothers. Strengthen them, Lord, for the enormous responsibility placed upon their shoulders. In Jesus' name. Amen.*"

Never Too Late

Marilyn Meberg

❥✖❥✖❥✖❥✖❥✖❥✖❥✖❥✖❥✖❥✖❥✖❥
There is a time for everything, and a season
for every activity under heaven.

ECCLESIASTES 3:1

"Come on, honey, you have to get out the door for school."
Hearing only silence, I popped into my eight-year-old's
room. Expecting to see Jeff hustling about in an effort to leave,
I was surprised to find him lying on his bed, hands behind his
head, staring at the ceiling.

"Sweetheart, are you okay? What are you doing just lying on
your bed?"

"I'm thinking."

"What are you thinking?"

"I'm thinking it's too late."

"Too late for what?"

"Going to school."

I sat down beside Jeff and wondered what was going on in
his mind. "Jeff, it really isn't too late. You have fifteen minutes.
I'll drive you so you won't have to walk; that way you'll have
plenty of time."

"No, Mama, it's too late for my mind, and it's too late for
my body."

Biting my lower lip to prevent a giggle, I asked him how long
he thought his mind and body would be in that state.

Sighing, he said, "Maybe all day."

Because he had never complained about this dire condition before, I let him stay home. We played a bit, went out to
lunch, and ate ice cream in the park. I worried that I might

be contributing to the let's-skip-school-and-play-instead syndrome. Jeff never complained again about his mind and body feeling too late but went off to school the next day on schedule.

Many times in my life I, too, have wondered if it simply weren't too late for my mind and body. Some days I've thought not one idea in my head was worthy of anything but the compost pile. And some days I've thought I should just drape my body over the compost pile as well.

I am, however, always inspired by stories of people who refused to think it was ever too late for their minds and bodies. George Dawson from Dallas, Texas, certainly fits that description.* At the age of ninety-eight, George decided to learn how to read. He had kept his illiteracy a secret for nearly ten decades, but encouraged by a teacher from a local adult education program, George, after two years in literacy class, has learned to read at the third-grade level and write his name in cursive script. His pride and pleasure over acquiring these skills is so infectious that many people are enrolling in the school just to receive encouragement from George or to be with him.

Another never-too-late story is that of Grandma Moses, who, at the age of seventy-eight, had her first showing of paintings she had done from picture postcards and Currier and Ives prints. The following year, she had fifteen one-woman art shows in both Europe and the U.S. At ninety-two, she wrote her autobiography, *My Life's History*. She received an honorary doctorate at age 100 and another at age 101. I suppose she figured she had done enough so she also died at age 101.

Closer to home is the story of Barbara Johnson, who wrote her first book when she was fifty. And now, at the age of seventy, she has more nonfiction books in print than just about anyone. She has given hope and encouragement to thousands of people through her Spatula Ministries and is a never-ending source of encouragement to my heart.

---

*"Happy," *People* (April 6, 1998), 112.

On a more personal note, my little Irish grandmother, at the age of 100, participated in a family reunion of her ten children, their spouses, and their children. The reunion was held on the old family farm where the ten "kids" had been raised. As they were organizing a baseball game to be played in the back field, my grandmother insisted on playing. When she hit a fly ball high into left field, her eldest son offered to run bases for her. "Are you kidding, Basil?" she snorted. "You're eighty years old," and off she trotted. She lived to be 103.

God has created within all human beings a tremendous drive to survive and a capability to succeed to the level of our God-given gifts. Isn't it fantastic to realize that most of us have barely tapped into our potential? We could be creating and contributing so much more.

What keeps us from living out that potential? Do you suppose a few of us are lying on our beds with our hands behind our head and thinking, *It's too late for my mind, and it's too late for my body.*

"Lord Jesus, don't let me miss what you have for me because I may have lost confidence in myself or in your enablement. May I be settled into the truth that I can indeed do all things through Christ who strengthens me. Then, Lord, softly push me out there; I promise I won't just lie on the bed. Amen."

Over and Over
Thoughts Worth Repeating

Here a Verse, There a Verse
Luci Swindoll

Do your best to present yourself to God as one approved,
a workman who does not need to be ashamed and who
correctly handles the word of truth.

2 TIMOTHY 2:15

*O*ne evening at dinner with a group of Dallas Seminary students, I was exchanging favorite Bible verses with them. A third-year student said, "Mine is 1 Chronicles 26:18."

I couldn't imagine what that was, so I quickly asked, "What is it?"

"'At Parbar westward, four at the causeway, and two at Parbar.'"

I thought for a moment, not wanting to seem like a dunce in the presence of a theologian. Finally, I had to admit it made no sense to me. "Is that *it?*" I questioned. "What does it *mean?*"

His answer was classic. "Who knows?" We all laughed hysterically.

I was reminded of the times I've talked about the favorite verse of single women: "If any man will come after me, let him ..." (Matthew 16:24 KJV). Now, mind you, if you read the verse in its entirety, the meaning changes drastically. But take it out of context, and it makes a very different point.

Once I printed a verse from Matthew 23 on a little watercolor I painted for a friend. The portion of the verse I used says, "... You travel over land and sea to win a single convert ..." (verse 15). That verse fits precisely the message I wanted to convey to my soul-winning friend. However, in proper context, you realize in that passage Jesus actually was condemning the Pharisees' action. He called them hypocrites because they were converting people to their own pharisaical ways, *not* the gracious ways of God.

These harmless exchanges of verses' meanings are fun, but sometimes it goes way beyond humor. How many times have we heard people *seriously* quote Scripture or use a verse to their own advantage rather than for its intended meaning? They *believe* what is lifted out of context, and that's dangerous!

God imparts his commands, plans, and ideas with specificity. There's no mixed message in what he's saying. But when I believe bits and pieces of Scripture, removed from their frame of reference, I run the chance of living in a dream world, waiting for things to happen according to my preference. Isaiah 55:8–11 (TLB) says:

> *This plan of mine is not what you would work out, neither are my thoughts the same as yours! For just as the heavens are higher than the earth, so are my ways higher than yours, and my thoughts than yours. As the rain and snow come down from heaven and stay upon the ground to water the earth, and cause the grain to grow and to produce seed for the farmer and bread for the hungry, so also is my Word. I send it out and it always produces fruit. It shall accomplish all I want it to, and prosper everywhere I send it.*

Oh, my, that's beautiful and ever so true! Become a student of Scripture. Know what it teaches. Believe what it says. Understand what it means. Impart its truth to others. When we share the Bible with others, we are giving them *life* . . . wonderful words of *life!* We're not just making suggestions for living; we're offering individuals a new way to think, act, feel, and live. It's not here a verse, there a verse. *In context,* it's a new way to understand life. God's way.

"*Sing them over again to me, Lord, wonderful words of life. Let me more of their beauty see, wonderful words of life. Amen.*"

Lastly

Patsy Clairmont

✘❤✘❤✘❤✘❤✘❤✘❤✘❤✘❤✘❤✘❤
So the last will be first, and the first will be last.

MATTHEW 20:16

Something about a last word is tasty. It's like the maraschino cherry sitting atop a hot fudge sundae—a pleasing, final touch. But, like the cherry, we often could have done without it.

The dictionary says *last* means "final." Whenever I pulled my mom's rubber-band emotions taut, she would threaten, "This is the last time I'm going to tell you." I usually could weigh by the tone of her voice if she meant really last or just close to last. Sometimes I called it right and sometimes . . . well, let's just say she left a final impression.

Then there's the last straw. "Okay, I've had it! That was the last straw!" We pitchfork this barnyard threat toward others to let them know their pigs have swilled in our mud for the last time, and we're calling in Oscar Mayer.

And what about the last laugh? Doesn't that have a rather odious sound? It makes a person want to hire rear guards to protect oneself from the stinging guffaws of a spiteful comedian. The last laugh sounds like a concoction of revenge with a twist of sardonic humor. Funny? Probably not, and lethal to swallow.

The last hurrah speaks of another final moment. Now, that one makes me feel melancholy. It's as if we're suggesting not only that the party is over, but also that we'll never be invited to another. Then again, it could mean we're about to leave something truly memorable, and we're adding an exclamation point to the festivities. Hurrah! I like that.

The last minute is how I live most of my life. I tend to down-shift when I should be accelerating and vice versa. This on-the-edge habit leaves me breathless, frustrated, and a little ditzy (and a little can go a long way). For some reason, in those last minutes, reality thumps me upside the head, and life finally comes into focus, which leaves me scurrying to catch up.

An important last for me is last names. I love my last name, Clairmont. I think it's so French, so romantic. My maiden name was McEuen. Good, strong name but not very, uh, poetic. In high school my best friend was Carol McEachern. When we would meet new folks, and they would ask us our names, our response caused laughter. We were accused of having made up our names. Trust me, if we had, we would have created far more Hollywood-ish or fairy tale-ish ones. On second thought, had we not had those names, we might never have become school chums (we sat in class alphabetically), and then we would never have enjoyed forty years of invaluable friendship.

How about the last dance? When Les and I were young, we promised to save that for each other. Our commitment still stands thirty-six years later.

"Last leg" is a phrase you hear every now and then. It suggests having used up all the other options, which is a sad state to be in, and one I hope to avoid.

Then there's the Last Supper, which for our Lord was tinged with sadness as he tried to prepare himself and his disciples for the ordeal before them. But the Last Supper has become the Lord's Supper for us, and while it reminds us of our sorrowful, sinful state, it also causes us to recall he who gave us reason to celebrate.

Some say we are living in the last days. I'm not prophetic, but I'm also not blind. Many scriptural signs point to our living in the closing chapter of history. But since the Lord's timing and ours are often so different, I'm not holding my breath. In fact, my heart's longing is that my last breath (whether at his coming or my leaving) be one of praise to him who gave his life and who gave me life.

If you could choose what your last will (carefully chosen act) and testament (words that testify to the heart of your life) would be, what would you pick?

"Jesus, you are the first and the last. You are the Alpha and Omega. You spell out meaning for our existence. And you are the one who will have the last word. Come quickly, Lord Jesus. Amen."

The Whole World in His Hands

Barbara Johnson

✖♥✖♥✖♥✖♥✖♥✖♥✖♥✖♥✖♥✖♥✖♥

May the favor of the Lord our God rest upon us;
establish the work of our hands for us—
yes, establish the work of our hands.

PSALM 90:17

Do you remember when every house had a clothesline and the "hand work" that went into washing those fresh-air-scented linens? How about the toasty feel of a wood fire burning first thing in the morning? In those days the ingredients for a good meal were grown in a garden and simmered for flavor all day.

Would you trade a modern convenience or two for one of those old-fashioned "luxuries"? Or were they all just too much trouble, taking too much time?

Something about handmade things brings serenity. They represent more than tedious hours or backbreaking work. I think they are to our souls what water is to a fish—the context in which to thrive. The soul thrives, as Ralph Waldo Emerson said, on "a little fire, a little food, and an immense quiet."

Would Martha Stewart agree? I'm not certain she's into the soul of things, but she's a woman who knows how to use her hands!

The problem is, when I try to copy Martha's style, I end up with one nerve left ... and someone is bound to get on it! Wanting a Currier and Ives holiday, I end up with "As the World Turns." I believe if you show me a woman whose home is always ready for company, I'll show you a woman who is too tired to entertain.

I want the handmade life but fall far short of soulful serenity. How to make both work? While Martha Stewart excels in the work of her hands, I ask myself, *What would Jesus do—with his hands—to bring graciousness and love to this world?*

Jesus would express welcome in a handshake and offer unconditional love in a hug. He would sit and listen, holding somebody else's hands folded in his own. He would wrestle fishing nets from the sea, tickle a kid, carve a beautiful piece of wooden furniture. I bet he knew how to paint, put a house together, build an altar, plant a garden, and give a back rub. If this kind of handmade love is freely given in a home, Jesus' presence will be felt there.

Use your hands to express humor, articulate a joke, elaborate a funny story. I used my hands for fun times when I was raising my four boys. From Jell-O fights to backyard baseball games, humor reminds children that adults can let down their guard. We don't always have to take ourselves so seriously.

Use hands to embrace precious moments, too. Caress a baby's cheek, stroke an arm, dry a tear. Spread hope in a hand around a shoulder, pick up someone who has fallen down, give the thumbs-up sign.

God gave us hands to give and to receive his blessings. Think of all the intricate and amazing things you do with your hands all day long: The way your fingers work together kneading bread or work separately to type a note. Your thumbs can grip a heavy object or stroke a kitten. The palm of your hand can rub a kink out of someone's back or smooth a fevered forehead.

Next time you hold a person's hands in yours, take a second to give those hands an extra squeeze. At the table, bless the food and the hands that prepared it. At bedside, fold your hands to pray. Use them lifted in worship or outstretched to reach for the moon. At the end of the day, put your hands to rest for work well done.

We can't all be Marthas, making candles from scratch, weaving our own baskets, or mixing our own dyes. But we are the hands of Jesus in this world. And that's far more important work.

"Jesus, I want to use my hands the way you used yours to heal and lift and resurrect lost things in people's lives. I pray the compassion I feel in my heart will find its way to my fingers. Amen."

Hey...It's Not My Fault!

Marilyn Meberg

✗❤✗❤✗❤✗❤✗❤✗❤✗❤✗❤✗❤✗❤
I acknowledge my transgressions.

PSALM 51:3 KJV

He's two-and-a-half years old, utterly adorable, and already has perfected the fine art of scapegoating. To my knowledge, no one has hunkered down with my grandson and explained the age-old practice of blaming others for his misdeeds. He seems to have taken to it quite naturally and, incidentally, does it well.

For the past few months, Ian has started to blame me for many of his minor sins.

"Ian," his mother, Beth, would say, "who told you it was okay to hide Halloween candy under your pillow?"

"Maungya."

"Ian, where did you ever learn a word like that?"

"Maungya."

"Ian, you don't eat dessert before you've finished your dinner."

"Maungya does!"

Last week Beth called to fill me in on a rather harrowing experience she had had when Ian overdosed on his multiple vitamin pill. As she was folding laundry in the bedroom, Ian managed to crawl up to the shelf where the vitamins were stored and break into the childproof bottle. Then he sauntered into the bedroom and sidled up to her holding the half-empty container with his mouth crammed full of orange-flavored pills. Because excessive amounts of iron are toxic and fearing that Ian might well have consumed enough iron to be dangerous, she called Poison Control and was advised to give him a dose of Ipecac, which would induce vomiting within twenty minutes. The experience was not pleasant, but he tossed up the pills in a timely manner and was soon playing with his backhoe and dump truck in the sandbox.

As Beth detailed all of this for me, Ian insisted he needed to talk to me immediately. Taking the phone from his mother, he stated in a reprimanding voice, "Maungya, you only take one vitamin pill! Did you hear me, Maungya?" In a short time he seemed to feel satisfied that he had sufficiently taken me to task, so he handed the phone back to his mother and went on about his important business.

I have giggled over Ian's stern discipline of me ever since. I have also spun off into a reverie about the whole blaming tendency that seems to be inherent in all of us. I've tried to figure out Adam's age when he blamed Eve for his disobedience to God's law. I figure he had been on the earth fewer days than Ian had when Adam pulled the stunt that ruined perfection for all of us. But, of course, it wasn't just Adam who did the blaming; Eve blamed the serpent for sweet-talking her into munching the forbidden fruit.

Blaming, refusing to take responsibility, passing the buck— whatever we call it, it has an ancient history. Much as I hate to admit it, I, too, find myself eager to shirk responsibility for my various mistakes and shortcomings.

Just this week I was struggling with the temptation to wriggle out of responsibility for having missed a telephone radio interview about my new book. I wanted to do the interview; I simply forgot about it. When a couple of friends suggested we go to Houston's restaurant for their fabulous spinach-artichoke dip and chips, I was in the car before anyone else could put on her shoes.

The next day on a flight to a conference I found the interview confirmation sheet in my briefcase. Pondering the situation, I thought, *Do I call the station and confess that I was slathered to the elbows in spinach-artichoke dip at the exact time I was supposed to be talking to them?*

Though that's the truth, it doesn't make me look good. If I told them there must have been a mistake in dates and I thought I was supposed to do the interview next week ... If I told them my secretary didn't inform me, and I knew nothing about the interview in the first place ... If I said a power outage occurred and all the phone lines were down for six hours ...

The bottom line is the truth doesn't make me look good, but not telling the truth makes me feel bad. What does one do? Well ... one tells the truth, takes responsibility, looks bad but feels right morally. (Incidentally, I called the station and confessed. I waited for a cool reception to my irresponsible behavior. Instead, they warmly forgave me and set up another interview time. I like those people.)

Why do you suppose we're so eager to blame instead of claim? My assumption is that we simply hate to look bad about anything to anyone—even ourselves. We don't want to be the bad guy ... we want someone else to be.

Do you remember the term *scapegoat* in Leviticus 16? The custom was to have two goats. The first was sacrificed as a sin offering, and the second, the scapegoat, had the people's sins transferred to it by prayer and the laying on of hands. It's thought that the scapegoat was then taken into the wilderness never to be seen again.

How appealing. Put my "stuff" on the goat, send it away, and forget about it.

Of course, the symbolism is obvious as we realize that Christ became our sin bearer. He took on himself the sin of the world that we might become blameless. Great as that news is, I still have to take personal responsibility for my sin. I have to admit it to myself and then to God and do so without the usual excuses.

Having done this, I can stop blaming and start claiming. Claiming what? Forgiveness! Feeling forgiven instead of full of excuses leads to freedom. Thank God we don't need a scapegoat; we have Jesus.

"Lord Jesus, how graciously you provide for our every need. Thank you that because of the cross, I can truly be viewed as blameless in your sight. Enable me, Lord, to extend that kind of grace to myself. Enable me to extend that kind of grace to others. Amen."

Zsa Zsa Walsh

Sheila Walsh

✖❤✖❤✖❤✖❤✖❤✖❤✖❤✖❤✖❤✖❤✖❤✖

She is clothed with strength and dignity; she can laugh at
the days to come. She speaks with wisdom, and faithful
instruction is on her tongue. She watches over the affairs
of her household and does not eat the bread of idleness.
Her children arise and call her blessed.

PROVERBS 31:25–28

My mother is not a flashy woman. She has a quiet strength
and dignity that I love and admire. So don't look for
flashy clothes or sparkly earrings when you meet her. Unless,
of course, you happened to see her one particular night . . .

I was asked to sing one New Year's Eve at Fuller Theologi-
cal Seminary's banquet. Mom was staying with me at the time,
and we were discussing what she would wear.

"I'll just wear one of my nice dresses," she said.

"I think you'll feel funny, Mom, because everyone else will
be in evening dress. It's a very dressy night here in America,"
I argued. I'd actually only been to one New Year's Eve banquet before but had underdressed. All the other women had
looked like they had fallen off Macy's Christmas tree.

"Let me buy you an outfit, Mom. Please!"

I went to the local mall and tried to find just the right clothes
that would be pretty but not too much for my mom. I bought
a beautiful sequined jacket that sparkled under the store light
and would look lovely with a black evening skirt.

Mom tried it on and loved it. "I'd never have bought this
myself," she said, "but it's fun!"

I had to be out of town the night before the dinner; so Barry and my mom checked into the hotel near Fuller, and we arranged that I would come straight from the airport to meet them at the banquet.

I arrived in time but watched in horror as all the other ladies went into the dining area. Not a sequin in sight! Not a sparkle, not a glimpse of a glitter. They were all in conservative church dresses. I swallowed hard and went in to see if my mom had arrived yet or if I could stop her. But there she was, Zsa Zsa Walsh in all her glory, looking like an aircraft landing light.

I felt so bad about taking my mother out of her comfort zone and leaving her there like a demented Christmas ornament. But she has a great sense of humor, and we both got a good laugh out of the experience. She told me that one woman asked her if that's how Scottish women dress on New Year's Eve, at which point my mother nearly choked.

What amazed me was that Mom had a lovely evening anyway. She wasn't embarrassed or angry with me; she was her usual, wonderful self.

That's the kind of woman I want to be—secure in Christ, not in wearing the right outfit. Is your closet your security? Do you need a new outfit when a scary situation awaits you? What happens if you misjudge and end up overdressed or understated?

A quiet beauty that you can't buy in any mall graces a godly woman. To that kind of woman this child rises up and calls her blessed.

"Father God, thank you for godly women. Thank you for those who prize your favor more than fashion or fame. Help me to grow in beauty in your eyes. Amen."

No Coincidences
Thelma Wells

❌💜❌💜❌💜❌💜❌💜❌💜❌💜❌💜❌💜
Direct my footsteps according to your word.

PSALM 119:133

I'm amazed at the number of situations that seem to be coincidences—until I stop and take a look at the whole picture. For instance, I never thought of myself as an author until a set of circumstances started the pages to roll off the presses.

One of my business associates, without my knowledge, recommended me as a speaker for a national organization. I found out about it when the conference coordinator called to tell me I had been selected. When the time neared that I was to speak, the organization called my office and asked that my books be at the conference by a certain date.

"My books? Did she say, 'My books'?" I spouted to anyone who was within hearing. "I don't have *one* book, let alone *books*. Nobody told me you were supposed to be published to speak for this group. They want 'my books' in six weeks!"

My daughter Vikki was in the office at the time and immediately took the telephone from me. She wrote down the instructions on where the books should be delivered, agreed that I would have a book there on or before the date, hung up the phone, and handed me one of the greatest challenges of my life. "Write the book!" she said. "You know you have all the information you need. It's time to stop procrastinating and do it. You'll write on the plane, in your hotel room, everywhere you can. Send the information back to me and don't worry about the rest. You *will* have a book at the conference. You can do it; I know you can! Now, get on it!"

With Vikki's tenacity, my knowledge and determination, the help of other people who assisted on the project, and God's grace, the book was delivered by the required date. But this was no coincidence. God had placed the material for the book in my mind and heart several years before; the speaking engagement just prodded me to do the writing. God had lined up all the circumstances to make it happen. That was just the beginning, however.

The very day I released this first book, *Capture Your Audience Through Storytelling*, another publisher approached me about writing my second book. I was startled. Write another book? I didn't think I had anything else to say. The publisher said, "I want you to write about the challenges and triumphs of your life."

Challenges and triumphs of my life? Who would want to hear about my life? He said he wanted me to write something Oprah would buy. Well, the thought was worth entertaining. So off I went into the world of book writing once again, with my daughter pushing and prodding me all the way. With the help of Jan Winebrenner, a wonderful writer, within eighteen months the second book, *Bumblebees Fly Anyway: Defying the Odds at Work and Home*, was released. No coincidence!

One of the administrators at New Life Clinics read the book and was convinced I needed to be a Women of Faith speaker—me, a person she had never met or heard of. When she approached me about speaking, the dates of the conferences were open on my calendar. No coincidence! As a result of being a speaker for this marvelous organization, I have written another book released March 1998, *God Will Make a Way*.

I was fifty-two years old when I wrote my first book. Now, at fifty-seven, I have either written or coauthored six books. This writing frenzy all started with a friend suggesting me as a speaker for a conference. And the "coincidences" go on.

I was standing in line with two friends to board an airplane in Salt Lake City when a lady and her daughter noticed my purple and white Women of Faith tote bag. The mother asked if we had attended a conference, adding that they had been to one in Lakeland, Florida, the previous year.

"We've been trying to contact one of the speakers," she said. Then she looked at me and said, "The bee! The bee! You're the one! You're the one with the bumblebee pins! You're the one we've been trying to locate for more than three weeks!"

Would you believe the mother and daughter's seats on the plane were two seats from ours?

As you look back over the circumstances of your life, can you discern the carefully planned patterns that at first looked like coincidences? Situations don't always follow our plans, but God orchestrates our lives nonetheless—sometimes to a tune we hear only faintly.

"Help me, Lord, to relinquish my life to you. Be Lord over my career, family, friends, talents, skills, abilities, ideas, desires, and prosperity. Enable me to remember that you have ordered my steps and that you will bring to pass what you have planned. As I survey my life, keep me mindful that, while I'm amazed at what you have done, in many ways, you have just begun. Amen."

Never Cage Joy

Barbara Johnson

✗♥✗♥✗♥✗♥✗♥✗♥✗♥✗♥✗♥✗♥✗♥✗♥

Then he touched their eyes and said, "According to your
faith will it be done to you."

MATTHEW 9:29

The story is told of a Civil War battle in which a beautiful
Southern mansion was used as a field hospital by the Union
army. The plantation itself was a bloody battlefield, but the matron
of the house refused to seek shelter elsewhere. She stayed in her
home to organize medical supplies and help wounded enemy sol-
diers. She wiped their brows as they died. In the midst of this bru-
tality, her courage and kindness was a testimony of grace.

Like this woman, but certainly in a less literal way, I have
faced brutal circumstances that took possession of things I held
dear and turned my life into a bloody mess. Unlike this woman,
I didn't always respond graciously.

Sometimes I was slow to realize that my trials didn't define
me. But eventually, I learned I am free, in Jesus' name, to behave
with mercy regardless of my circumstances. I learned to ask,
What can I learn here? How can I help others?

And when the sun is shining on my rooftop, when things
are going my way? The same rules apply—and are just about
as hard to learn. Our blessings don't define us either. We can't
count on blessings; we have to hold them loosely. But we are
free to behave with grace because of who we are, not what we
have or what happens to us.

At times I've been like the little girl who set off to search
for the bluebird of happiness. She looked in the past but couldn't
find it. She looked to the future but couldn't find the bird. Then

she looked in the present. When the bluebird of happiness appeared, she was happy. She felt inspired. She went out to do good while the bird sang a beautiful song in the treetops.

After a while, the little girl grew afraid. *What if I lose the bluebird of happiness?* she wondered. *What if it flies away?* So she built a cage of bamboo sticks, filled it with seed and pretty branches, and tucked the bird away for safekeeping. But the bird grew quiet, singing less and less until it stopped altogether. Eventually, the bluebird of happiness died.

The little girl learned that joy can't be contained but must be free to come and go, which it will—just as trouble is never permanent. In the Lord, I am free of circumstance, whether good or bad. At the beginning of each day I make two choices: first, to accept trouble if it comes and to look for opportunities to do good in spite of how I feel. Second, never to cage joy if it alights on my shoulder or lands in my lap. I will set the bluebird of happiness free to bless some other person's life. And sometimes the bluebird comes back to rest in my tree.

A neighbor of mine had lots of cats (at one time forty of them!). Since she was ninety-four years old, I sort of looked after her, doing her shopping, taking her to the doctor, and keeping her supplied with kitty litter. She died recently, and to my surprise, she left me two gorgeous diamond rings. That was totally unexpected. Thrilled, I had them sized and wore them proudly. Then someone pricked my happiness by saying, "Anyone with a tax-exempt, nonprofit ministry shouldn't wear expensive diamonds like that!"

The cutting words made me feel bad for a while. Then I let them go. They don't define me. I am free in Jesus. The diamonds? They were a bluebird of happiness passed along to me by a dear friend, and in that way, they were a gift from Jesus himself. (My husband, Bill, says I earned every sparkle in the rings for all the cat doo-doo I cleaned up.) For as long as I have the rings, they'll remind me of how God brings unexpected joy into my life. Should I lose them for any reason, that's okay, too.

So if you see me wearing a couple of dazzling diamonds, let them be an encouragement to *you!* The Lord wants to bless you, unearned and unexpected. Accept the doo-doo and the dazzle that comes your way—you're bound to experience both!

"Heavenly Father, although our lives are full of the unexpected, you are solid and sure. Help me to make my way through the mud puddles and to skip on mountaintops, taking things as they come. Bless me as the battles rage or the bluebird sings. Amen."

---

*Leo Buscaglia, *Bus Nine to Paradise* (New York: SLACK, Inc., 1986), 126.

A Fluffy, Vulnerable Heart

Luci Swindoll

You will be made rich in every way so that you can be
generous on every occasion, and through us your
generosity will result in thanksgiving to God.

2 Corinthians 9:11

*E*veryone in the world needs to know Andrea Grossman.
She's just *that* kind of person. If you don't know her, stop
what you're doing, and come meet her now. I'll introduce you!

She's a devoted mother, a successful businesswoman, an
exceptional entrepreneur, a committed Christian, a celebrated
artist, a sweetheart, and a great friend. In short, Andrea is One
Fabulous Woman. Maybe you've used some product from Mrs.
Grossman's Paper Company and have not known the genius
behind the label.

Many words describe Andrea, but my favorite is *generosity*.
I have never in my life known a more generous individual.
Behind all her generosity is the love of God.

The great Chinese philosopher, Lao Tzu, wrote, "Kindness
in words creates confidence, kindness in thinking creates pro-
foundness, and kindness in giving creates love."* With a spirit
of kindness, Andrea gives confidence, thoughtfulness, and love.

Recently, five friends accompanied me to Andrea's office.
We'll be talking about that forever. (In fact, Patsy Clairmont
talks about it in this book!) None of my friends knew Andrea
when we first arrived, and I couldn't wait to give them that
pleasure. When we left seven delightful hours later, we were all

bonded for life. We departed with our arms and hearts filled with the gifts of her giving.

An artist by talent and training, Andrea was asked several years ago to draw a little red heart for a friend. The heart became a sticker, the first of thousands of stickers and sticker products she has designed.

"I didn't want to draw just any old heart," Andrea said. "I wanted it to pulsate. You know, a fluffy, vulnerable heart." I knew exactly what she meant. I've since come to realize that heart is more than a drawing; it's a metaphor for Andrea's life.

Her heart reflects love toward her employees, vendors, and customers. Her spirit of generosity extends to those less fortunate than she—from hiring the handicapped to providing product for rest homes and children's centers.

The giving never stops. I remember the time Andrea gave crisp $100 bills to her employees because the month had been especially good for the company.

I think of Andrea Grossman when I read 2 Corinthians 9:11. In fact, her life showcases the whole passage from verses 6 through 15. If you really want to meet this woman, sit down now and read those verses, start to finish.

Here's the beauty of that passage: It says that, when we are given riches all the time, that happens so we can be generous all the time. When we're generous all the time, people see it and thank God all the time.

God gives to us, we give to others, others praise him, and then he starts over. It's a wonderful cycle. Eugene Peterson calls it "the plain meaning of the message of Christ."

I see that "plain meaning" in Andrea. God has given to her, she gives to others, we praise God, and he gives her more to give. It all starts with cultivating a fluffy, vulnerable heart. Thank you, Andrea, for *your* generosity. You make that passage come alive.

"Heavenly Father, you have been exceedingly generous to us, your children. May we not hold back one single gift of your giving. Help us give and give and give some more—our time, energy, and money, so that others will see your love through us. Amen."

I See … Sorta

Patsy Clairmont

✗♥✗♥✗♥✗♥✗♥✗♥✗♥✗♥✗♥✗♥✗♥✗♥

The lamp of the body is the eye.

MATTHEW 6:22 nasb

The last time I ordered new glasses I had no-glare coating put on the lenses. That way, when I'm on a platform speaking, I don't refract light like some kind of Star Wars invader every time I turn my head. That no-glare stuff really works great, but as in most enhancements, there is a side effect—my lenses smudge easily. In fact, I'm constantly viewing life through thumbprints, which eliminates a lot of life's little details like steps, curbs, and hedges.

Besides the threat of being tripped up, I have to crinkle my face to see through the fog (like I need another crop of deep-set lines in my face). But I think the most disturbing aspect of this smudge factor is that everyone else notices my lenses are a smeared mess. It's sort of like the junk I hide under my bed. I know it's there, but I don't want anyone else to view it. People even offer to clean my glasses for me. How embarrassing. Actually, their efforts only seem to rearrange the design of the smudges. The last set looked similar to the streaming-star effect of going to hyper speed on Han Solo's Millennium Falcon. I'm constantly asked, "How do you see through them?" Well, I don't know. I guess I've adjusted to people looking like walking trees.

Tonight I walked into an optometry store and asked the attendants to remove the no-glare treatment. They looked at me as if I had said, "My name is Chewbacca."

The first gal shot a glance at the other and said, "Is it possible to reverse this process?"

The other one shrugged her shoulders, pleading ignorance as she headed toward me. Staring at the glasses perched atop my nose, she quipped, "How do you see through those?" Here we go again. "Let me clean them for you," she offered. I could see that one coming.

Meanwhile, her cohort had chatted with the specialist in the back who said he could only do the reversal if I had bought the glasses from their store, which I hadn't. Out of frustration, the girl handed back my glasses, telling me they wouldn't come clean (surprise, surprise). She recommended I invest in new lenses, which (surprise, surprise) they could do for me for a little less than a Princess Leia face-lift.

I left in my usual fog, promising to return if I could see my way clear to buy new spectacles. Then I stumbled through the mall wondering how life would look if I stepped out from behind my cumulus clouds.

There are some advantages in not seeing clearly, you know. I mean, even the little I can see clearly in the morning mirror hasn't been all that wonderful. To see clearly could be more of a reality check than I'm ready for. If my house truly came into focus, I might have to do something radical—like vacuum. Not to mention the obligation I'd feel to weed the garden, wash the windows, and polish the silver. Nah, on second thought, who needs new glasses?

Hmm, I believe blessed fog may be a fairly common approach to life (like a cold). For instance, have you ever paced wide circles around a scale lest you step on the thing and see your Social Security number pop up? Or have you ignored a health issue lest the doctors install R2D2 parts in your anatomy? Or maybe you've been tiptoeing around an issue between you and someone else, hoping it would vaporize while, in reality, it grows more complex with each passing day.

"Jesus, forgive us when we resist looking honestly at our lives. For unwillingness to face the truth will lead us far from you. Give us the courage to press into reality. We don't want to live in denial. Denial has to do with darkness and you, dear Savior, have called us to be children of the light. Change our lenses so we might not only see others and ourselves more accurately but also so we might lift our eyes (lamps) and focus on you. Amen."

Take Me Back

Marilyn Meberg

✖♥✖♥✖♥✖♥✖♥✖♥✖♥✖♥✖♥✖♥✖♥✖♥
I the LORD do not change.

MALACHI 3:6

*O*ne of my favorite local stores is an English import shop that specializes in delicate bone china cups, teapots, little plates, and a myriad of other items crucial to the civilized preparation and drinking of tea. I was gingerly fingering a set of tiny Wedgwood butter dishes several weeks ago when the sound of twangy music began to penetrate my consciousness.

I paused, listened more closely, and thought, *Well, surely I'm not hearing "Church in the Wildwood." That doesn't fit this store.* "Shall We Gather at the River," "Nothing But the Blood of Jesus," and "O for a Thousand Tongues to Sing" followed.

I walked over to the very proper British owner and told her I loved the CD playing in the background. With her clipped, precise accent, she said, "Yes, isn't it quaint? We play it all the time."

The proprietor didn't seem to care about the message in those old hymns but instead seemed moved by the music's sounds and rhythms. The CD, entitled *Appalachian Memories*, featured handcrafted instruments: acoustic guitar, mandolin, Dobro, Autoharp, high-string guitar, and bass.

I was equally charmed by the sounds and rhythms; so forgetting all about the Wedgwood, I bought the CD and beat a hasty retreat home. It sounded even better on my sound system, and I found myself toe-tapping, grinning, and singing along from a wellspring of joy deep within me.

Just as the group and I were at the height of volume in "Love Lifted Me," Luci tapped at my window and wandered in. She

137

watched me for a minute, looking perplexed and slightly uncomfortable.

Snapping off the CD player, I said, "I love that sound. Something about it pleases me way down to the core of my being!"

"It pleases you," she said uncertainly. Apparently, the music didn't have that effect on her. "Why?"

"As best I can figure, it takes me back to the little churches I grew up in."

Looking at the picture and title of the CD, she said, "You grew up in the Appalachians?"

"No . . . you know that."

"Well, what draws you?"

"I guess it's the Dobro!"

Laughing, Luci suggested that neither of us had ever heard of a Dobro, which, of course, was true. Nevertheless, every time I pop that CD into my machine, I grin and tap—and Luci disappears.

I think much of the soul-satisfying appeal comes from merely hearing those old hymns without orchestral adornment—just the straightforward, even plain sounds, somewhat like those Mrs. Farr used to coax out of the pump organ on Sunday mornings.

I experience a longing from time to time for a porch, a rocker, and a dog. I'd even like to look over at a barn with hay in it and cows languidly chewing their cud in the foreground. Maybe a few chickens could peck about, making those funny throat sounds that must mean something to their relatives. And, of course, parked over by the side of the house would be a dirty blue pickup truck with the windows rolled down. Aunt Bess, with her straw hat slightly askew, would sit in the truck all day just in case someone decided to drive to town.

I can picture all this so vividly because I've just described the farm that belonged to Leonard and Georgia Parker in Amboy, Washington, where I grew up. Their adult daughter, whom everyone called Aunt Bess, had the IQ of a six-year-old. She never seemed discouraged about anything. Every day she would sit in the pickup and walk back into the house each evening in time for supper. In the event someone went somewhere, she got to go along. Going or staying never seemed to alter her pleasure with each day.

The appeal of *Appalachian Memories* is that it takes me back to my childhood, a time when my life was less hurried and much less sophisticated. That rich and spiritually sweet world was peopled by folk who loved Jesus, loved each other, and let me drive their tractor.

Even though times and surroundings have changed, one thing never changes—Christ. He loved me then; he loves me now. He blessed me then, and he blesses me now. He is the solid rock upon which I stand now and forever. I love that constancy. What spiritual security we have. It's better than *Appalachian Memories*.

Hey, hear that sound? That's the Dobro and Autoharp playing "Victory in Jesus." Come on, let's tap, grin, and sing! We'll do it before Luci pops by.

Actually, I'll let you in on a little secret. She confessed she felt a bit dewy-eyed when she heard "At the Cross." Her daddy played a sweet Autoharp in his day. I think the sound took her back.

"Lord, how comforting to know you are always there, living your life of love and victory through us no matter where we are or how old we are. You have promised to never leave us. Thank you for the security of your continual presence and your unchanging nature. Amen."

Overalls

Covered in Righteousness

×♥×♥×♥×♥×♥×♥×♥×♥×♥×♥×♥×♥×♥×♥

At Your Service
Luci Swindoll

O LORD, God of Abraham, Isaac and Israel, let it be known
today that you are God in Israel and that I am your
servant and have done all these things at your command.

1 KINGS 18:36

About my purse. I only carry what is absolutely essential in
there. Only what I really need. Or might need. In addition to typical items one might expect such as a billfold, checkbook, notepad, and coin purse, I carry other important stuff. For
example: hand cream; tissues; instant antibacterial hand gel;
electronic organizer; and leather cases for postcards, stamps,
credit cards, pens, Post-it notes, and sunglasses. Oh, and I have
to have my Day-Timer, glasses cleanser, and a small black satchel
crammed full of other important paraphernalia such as lipstick,
mirror, toothpicks, nail file, international clock, hole punch, a
Swiss Army knife with its twenty-six "tools," and a booklet that
tells folks how to accept the Lord. I don't carry the kitchen sink,
but I do have everything it takes to repair one. Okay, so I have
back pain. I also have what I need when I need it.

If you think my purse is full, try looking in my dresser drawers! Barbara Johnson sent me a handheld mirror not long ago,
which I store in one of my drawers. Every time I open that
drawer, the mirror lets out a wolf whistle. No matter how bad
I look or how low I feel, here comes this wonderful "woeeee-
weoooo." Makes me perk right up. That whistle always cheers
an otherwise dull day. Other drawers have equally fascinating
treasures. I'm bonded to my stuff, and everybody knows it.

I like things that serve my needs. And I want access to them
conveniently, immediately, and continuously.

Recently, I opened two small packets of Bayer aspirin. Inside was a flat, folded paper cup. When you pressed its tiny sides, it opened so you could put water inside and drink from it. I was ecstatic. I put that adorable cup right in my purse. I might need it sometime. Printed on it were the words, "Another innovative idea for 'people on the go' from Mechanical Servants, Inc."

How clever. Somebody's newfangled idea to meet a need. My kitchen is full of such gadgets. Knife sharpeners. Mixers. Bread machines. Blenders. Cheese graters. Lemon squeezers.

And the bathroom! Toothbrushes, night-lights, multispray showerheads, magnifying mirrors, and mobile phone. Every day we call on our mechanical servants, and we want them *now*.

I looked up the word *servant* in my concordance and found it's used more than four hundred times in Scripture. Of course, those servants were in the human rather than mechanical form, but the idea is the same. They did the bidding of the one with whom they were aligned. And repeatedly God commended them. Abraham was called the servant of God. And Moses. And David. In fact, David, as a servant of the Lord, wrote in Psalm 119:124–25:

> Deal with your servant according to your love
> and teach me your decrees.
> I am your servant; give me discernment
> that I may understand your statutes.

I want to be God's servant. When he asks me to do something, I want to be responsive. Instantly and always. My desire is to be as ready and convenient for his use as my stuff is for mine. He has equipped me with all the tools I need to be used for his purpose. There's nothing mechanical about it.

"*Father, give me the spirit of a servant, a heart that is more giving, loving, and attentive to the needs of others than to those of myself. Will you help me with that? Amen.*"

I Said I Was Sorry!

Thelma Wells

✘♥✘♥✘♥✘♥✘♥✘♥✘♥✘♥✘♥✘♥✘♥

For I will forgive their wickedness and
will remember their sins no more.

JEREMIAH 31:34

When my two-and-a-half-year-old granddaughter Vanessa
visited my home recently, she was having such a good
time she forgot to mention she needed to use the potty. Her
mother, aunts, cousin, and grandmother could see into the
kitchen where Vanessa was industriously playing. Most of us
noticed the same thing at the same time.

Vanessa was standing with a look on her face that said, "Oh,
oh, I'm going to catch it now!"

Tina, her mother, looked at Vanessa and exclaimed, "What
did you do?"

Vanessa answered with the angelic innocence of a child,
"I'm sorry."

"Vanessa, I thought I told you to tell me when you want to
use the bathroom. You're too special to be wetting on yourself."

While Tina continued to fuss, Vanessa, a fifty-pound, round
mulatto with Shirley Temple curls swirling on her head, again
sweetly said, "I'm sorry!"

That didn't seem to faze her mother. She kept on fussing.
"Vanessa, I don't understand how you can be so good when
we're at home, but as soon as we go somewhere, you forget to
tell me." On and on she lectured.

Eventually, Vanessa grew sick of the endless discussion of her
behavior. She was standing in a puddle, and her panties were
wet. Everybody was looking at her and listening to Tina go

145

on. So Vanessa widened her brown eyes, put her right hand where her hip would be if she had a waistline, slightly bent her left knee, and said to her mother with all the disgust of a disgruntled ten-year-old, "I *said*, I'm sorry!"

Oh, my goodness. All of us were trying not to laugh. We had compassion for Vanessa's dilemma, but she had broken the rules.

How often do we ignore God's rules for our lives because we're too busy, too involved in our own thing, don't believe, make up our own rules, or choose to be downright rebellious? I can imagine God looking at us something like Tina looked at Vanessa and saying, "My child, how many times does it take to convince you that my way is the right way? My timing is the perfect timing? My authority is the ultimate authority? My instructions will lead you to a way that has been designed for your good. Why don't you obey me?"

As he questions us, if we're sensitive to listen to his admonishment, we're quick to say, "Father, I'm sorry!" Before the twinkling of an eye, he says, "Forgiven!"

Hallelujah, we don't have to listen to all that fussing! He knows when we mean what we say and when we don't. He is ready, willing, and able to forgive to the utmost without continuing to talk and talk and talk. Praise God for the power in the phrase, "I'm sorry!"

Do you and God need to have a little talk? I promise you it will be short if you go to him with a humble heart, saddened by your sin.

"Father God, I appreciate that when we fail to obey your rules and tell you how sorry we are, you listen with compassion and forgive us. Oh, what grace! Please accept my apology for the many times I have defied your authority and haven't followed the rules. Thank you for allowing us to say, 'I'm sorry.' Amen."

God's Garage Sale

Barbara Johnson

✖❤✖❤✖❤✖❤✖❤✖❤✖❤✖❤✖❤✖❤

But seek first his kingdom and his righteousness, and all
these things will be given to you as well.

MATTHEW 6:33

Did you ever go to God's garage sale? I did. I found a lot of useful things at bargain rates, and a few priceless items to be had for a song!

The first thing I came across was a used reputation, somewhat tarnished. Brushing off the dust, I peered at the surface's blackness. *Could it be restored?* I wondered. Convinced a little spit and polish, a healthy dose of repentance, and a dab of forgiveness would make it good as new, I decided to take it home.

Next, I stumbled over a box of rusty evangelism opportunities. They looked as if they had been lying in an attic for a long, long time. There was a smile for a downhearted store clerk, left brittle and stiff. Goodies for a needy family that never quite made it to their doorstep. A coupon for baby-sitting that had never been offered. An invitation to Sunday school that had never been spoken. The opportunities had been neglected but weren't beyond repair. I decided to try rejuvenating their power with a little prayer.

Then, in the corner, I spied a suit of armor that looked as if it might fit me. I'd been needing some protection. I picked up the belt and buckled it on; the truth fit perfectly. A sturdy breastplate—although a bit weathered—felt just right. With the shoes on my feet, I was ready to meet friends and enemies alike. A shield was dented with arrow pits. A helmet was in excellent shape, looking as if it had never been used. Last, the sword; it had never lost its edge. I grabbed the whole box. One never knows when one might need to stand against all odds and the powers of darkness, too.

I took my stuff to the table to pay for it all and found a talent or two lying uselessly to the side. "What in the world are these?" I asked.

"Oh, just some unwanted stuff," the cashier told me. "The gift of helps, the gift of compassion. The owner left them behind when she went off in search of fame and fortune."

I decided to buy those, too.

Just as I was ready to leave, I spied a splintered piece of wood, stained with blood and pocked with what looked like nail holes. It reminded me that God so loved the world he didn't send a committee. I picked up the wooden cross and was told, "That's in the freebie box; it won't cost you a thing."

Once home with my garage sale treasures, I laid them on my kitchen counter and began to think how I might use them in my own or other people's lives. It didn't take much. A little sanding, some elbow grease, a new coat of paint, and sealer. I've learned through the years to get by the old-fashioned way: use it up, wear it out, make it do, or do without.

But I also know the things of the Spirit last forever. The things that others rejected have become the cornerstones of my life. They may be broken but are worth mending when the Lord's grace is the glue.

From now on, I'll always brake for God's garage sale. How about you?

"Father, thank you for the cache of spiritual treasure you have given each of us. Help me recognize their worth and to remember that there isn't anything you can't make new again. Even me. Amen."

Something Worth Holding On To
Sheila Walsh

❌❤❌❤❌❤❌❤❌❤❌❤❌❤❌❤❌❤❌❤❌❤

What good is it for a man to gain the whole world,
yet forfeit his soul?

MARK 8:36

Good morning, sir."

The man heard his butler's voice through a foggy mind still numbed from the previous evening's party. Grunting, he turned over on his side and let the aroma of freshly brewed coffee waft over him. He slid out of the silk sheets and headed to the shower.

As he dried his hair, he looked at his reflection in the mirror. He was a short, balding man with clumsy features. His nose looked as if it had been put on in a last-minute rush and wasn't quite centered. He consistently ate too much and drank too much.

"I do because I can," he rationalized. Beneath the obscene displays of wealth, however, he was a very lonely man.

He had begun his business with one small pawnshop off the main strip in Las Vegas. As the desperate rushed through his doors looking for just enough money to win their fortunes, he gladly stroked their weakness. Within two years he had three stores, and now his empire stretched its tentacles in all directions.

As he dressed, he recalled a conversation from the night before with a young woman just as he was closing one of his shops. She had pawned her diamond engagement ring the previous evening. He guessed it to be worth about ten thousand dollars and had given her five hundred. Now she was back and in a panic. Her fiancé was coming into town that evening, and she needed her ring back.

"I have exactly five hundred," she said.

"Sorry, that's not going to cut it," he replied, shaking his head. "There's interest to be paid."

"It's all I have," she cried. "Here, take my watch."

"Sorry, ma'am. No can do." With that he had closed the door in her face.

Stupid woman, he thought, as he reached for his morning cup of coffee. *I love them all!*

After a quick breakfast he headed down the marble stairs and out the door to his car. "The stupid and desperate still flock to my door," he said with a smile as he handed over his takings to the bank's vice president. The executive didn't laugh.

"They're all jealous," the man reasoned.

He left the bank and drove down the strip. Blind to the grandiose buildings and the crowds, he was lost in private thoughts that had haunted him more and more lately. He had no real friends. He recognized in his more honest moments that what he chose to read as envy was more likely disgust.

He became aware that the traffic had come to a stop. He pressed on his horn, but nothing moved. He decided to get out to see what was happening. Being a short man, it was hard to look over the crowd so he climbed onto the hood of his car to get a better view. A man was in the middle of the strip, and a crowd had gathered around him.

At that moment the man turned to him and said, "Zacchaeus, I'd like to have lunch with you."

After Jesus had left his home, Zacchaeus had stopped by his store and then drove on to the Desert Motel. He knocked on a few doors until he finally found the woman he was looking for.

"What do you want?" she asked in disgust. "You have your pound of flesh."

"I want to give you your ring back, and if you would allow me, I'd consider it an honor to pay for your wedding."

Years later, Zacchaeus lay in a hospital bed, and his mind went back to that day of all days when he finally found what he was looking for in the eyes of Jesus of Nazareth.

"How are you feeling, Zacchaeus?" the woman by his bedside asked.

"Never better, Linda."

She had been part of that transforming day, too. Now she held his hand as he went to be with Christ. He had given away most of his money, but it was a rich man who died that day.

Zacchaeus's story unfolds a bit differently in the Scripture, but I've taken liberties with it to remind us how radical a tale it was.

Whatever you have in life, if you don't have a relationship with Jesus, you have nothing, absolutely nothing. No relationship or object will touch the ache inside your heart. That ache is the shape of eternity.

"I lift my heart to heaven in grateful songs of praise. For I have found my resting place in you, Ancient of Days. Amen."

Oops, I've Fallen

Patsy Clairmont

✗❤✗❤✗❤✗❤✗❤✗❤✗❤✗❤✗❤✗❤✗❤
Now therefore, if ye will obey my voice indeed, and keep
my covenant, then ye shall be a peculiar treasure unto me
above all people: for all the earth is mine.

Exodus 19:5 kjv

We definitely live in a fallen world. Why, just today I was
attacked by a doll. Not just any doll but one of my own.
I had her standing on my dresser top, and when I bent over to
slide open a drawer, she fell and beaned me on my noggin.
Her head is porcelain while mine, I thought, was granite. Evi-
dently my noodle is more the consistency of Silly Putty because
her head left a crater-sized indentation in my cranium. She
came down with such a thud it took me several minutes before
I could carry on.

Speaking of noodles, get this. In Japan a noodle museum is
all the rage. Honest. It's far more popular than the art muse-
ums, which are generally visited only by scholars.

Imagine if someone could combine the two. The "Mona
Lisa" could be done in rigatoni (be hard for her not to smirk).
Or picture "Whistler's Mother" trying to rock on a chair of mac-
aroni. (Next we'll be sticking a feathered hat on her.) Or how
about "The Girl with the Watering Can" being renamed "The
Girl with the Ravioli."

Actually, the noodle museum is dedicated to the ramen noodle, which I understand is as popular in Japan as hot dogs are
at Chicago's O'Hare Airport (more are sold there than anywhere
else in the country). In one year the Japanese wolf down enough
noodles at the museum's nine ramen shops to encircle the globe

five times. Wow! Imagine if it rained. It could give new meaning to wet noodle—although if it filled in the ozone hole that could be good.

I think the news proves daily how off our noodles we humans are. Our fallen condition is proclaimed continuously by our odd behavior. I think of individuals who have been featured on the ten o'clock news for scaling high-rise buildings in major cities. The Andes are one thing, but the World Trade Center? C'mon, what's that about? Or skydiving off the Space Needle. Spacey, if you ask me. But then, truth be known, I've done a few weird things myself.

I remember the time I wound my foot around my neck (I was much younger) in an attempt to duplicate a trick by a TV contortionist. I managed to slide my foot around the back of my neck, but when my toes hooked close to my ear, I couldn't unwind myself. It took just seconds to realize what an unnatural position this was so I yelled to my husband for help.

To suggest Les was amazed when he tromped into the room and saw his wife in a virtual knot would be to underestimate his incredulous response. "Hurry," I commanded, hoping to jolt him into action. It worked, and he dislodged my foot, releasing the pressure off my cramping leg. I appreciated his assistance but was a tad irritated at his incessant snickering during the unwinding process.

Of course, I remember the time Les fell two stories off a roof with two bundles of roofing tiles on his shoulder. Falling off a roof is not odd. What was odd was when he stood up after several moments of staring at the sky, picked up the bundles, and scaled his way back up to the roof to finish the job.

If it isn't dolls falling on us and knocking us silly, our own silly fascinations remind us that sometimes we let life get out of whack. All that points to our fallen nature. We just can't keep things in balance (or balanced on our dresser tops).

When in doubt about your need to be saved, just check what's out of place in your life. It could be decorations that won't stay put, interests that become fetishes, or some less-than-bright action you've taken. Fortunately, even if something falls on our noodle or if we fall on our behind, God's everlasting arms pick us up, and he embraces us with his loving-kindness.

"I don't know for sure, Lord, but I think we might be confused by your call for us to become peculiar people. We are fallen people with strange ways. Please deliver us from our bright ideas. Untie our noodley brains lest we become wise in our own eyes. Amen."

Life, Death, and Turtles

Marilyn Meberg

Jesus said, "Let the little children come to me."

MATTHEW 19:14

Y ou know, Elizabeth, I don't expect that child to live much beyond the age of six." My father, thinking I was safely out of earshot, made this dire prediction to my mother. He had just stopped the flow of blood from a deep cut to one of my knees and a cut on my right cheek, then he had successfully pulled out both front baby teeth, which had been dangling crookedly by thin membrane.

My four-year-old determination to fly like a bird had produced numerous other death-defying schemes, none of which was successful and all of which unsettled my parents. Each time they had rushed forward with bandages and Mercurochrome, wondering why they never saw me before I took my flying leaps.

As I lay on my bed obediently taking the rest for which I felt no need but recognized was purely for the benefit of my frazzled parents, I pondered my father's words. It took me awhile, but I ultimately figured out that if I lived to be six, that meant I had two more years to go. Actually, that seemed a lifetime to me. A lot of living was yet to be done, I reasoned, and if I died at six, well, so be it. I also decided that perhaps I'd focus my future energies on some goal other than flying.

I was five-and-a-half years old when Leroy Walker lumbered into my life. He was a turtle who had been tyrannizing Mrs. Boden's garden, and she said he could be mine if I simply promised to keep him away from her vegetables. That seemed an easy enough task so I committed to keeping Leroy in my yard. But somehow life ceased to be a pleasure for Leroy in spite of the various green delicacies I provided him. Within a short time, he died.

My horror at his death was not that I had lost a beloved pet but that in a few weeks I would be six years old. That turtle and I were going out together, and I wasn't ready! I ran into the house, throwing myself into my mother's arms and telling her I didn't want to die, that the whole idea scared me and I thought I was still too young for it.

After my mother assured me I wasn't going out at age six, she also assured me that death need not be something to fear. I would immediately be in God's presence whenever I died. Then we talked about how I could be assured I would go to heaven. When she explained to me that everyone in the world is born in sin and that sin is the part of you that wants to do the wrong thing, I felt not only a surge of understanding but also relief.

The idea of sin had never made sense to me until then. I knew full well something in me not only enjoyed doing the wrong thing but also sought it out.

A kid lived down the street from me who would do anything I suggested. One time I told him I was sure his mother would love it if he colored the wallpaper roses in the bathroom with her red lipstick. So he did and, of course, was in huge trouble as a result.

It bothered me that I would think up those kinds of things for him to do—that didn't seem to stop me, though. It had never occurred to me that my behavior was something everyone in the world experiences called "sin."

I figured my various flying schemes probably came from that sin root. I knew my parents didn't want me leaping off buildings, which was why I sneaked away to our neighbor's yard, which had an old garage I thought perfect as a launching pad. Neither my parents nor the neighbor had any idea I'd figured out how to open the gate that separated our properties. All of those schemes were tinged with that sense of wrongdoing, but now I had a name for the wrongdoing.

Even better, I learned there was a cure ... his name was Jesus. When I asked him to come into my heart and clean up the sin mess, I was thrilled and relieved. I never doubted that he came, and I never doubted that I needed him. I will always carry that propensity to want to do the wrong thing ... but now I will also always carry the cure within me.

Many times I've thought back to Leroy Walker and the pivotal role he played in my life. It's amazing to me that on his life and death rested my ultimate understanding about my own life and death. I was a little person to whom God sent a little messenger. He knew how to speak my language. I like that about him.

Perhaps God has designed a little messenger who will amble into your life with a pivotal message. How about that for an intriguing anticipation?

"Thank you, Lord, for your gentle teaching and tender presence; thank you that your welcome and forgiveness extend to all persons at all times and in all stages of development. Amen."

The Rabbi and I

Luci Swindoll

The grass withers and the flowers fall,
but the word of our God stands forever.

ISAIAH 40:8

We were practically twins. He was dressed in black from head to toe, as was I. He carried black luggage, just as I did. He was reading a book. Me, too. The primary difference was he had a long, gray, untrimmed beard that hung over the front of his coat. *That* I couldn't match.

We were sitting in the waiting room of the Palm Springs Airport anticipating our departure to Dallas-Ft. Worth, killing time before we boarded the plane. The morning was cold. Early February. After scrutinizing the surroundings, I opened my book. It was *Psalms*, a modern translation by Eugene Peterson. My twin opened his book, too ... the Old Testament, in Hebrew. I noticed out of the corner of my eye the hardback spine was worn and tattered and the pages well marked. My book was new and paperback. It cracked when I opened it.

I watched him ever so intently as he pored over the Scriptures, his aging fingers underlining the words he read. Suddenly we were more than dressed alike. We were kindred spirits. I, too, had spent years with God's Word ... maybe not as many as he, but at least five decades. The Scriptures gave direction to my parents as I was growing up, guidance to us as a family, credibility to my life choices. I've memorized and believed Bible verses from my earliest remembrance.

Obviously, this rabbi also knew where to go to hear God's voice. Coming from such diverse backgrounds, we shared this common bond. Because the Scriptures never change, the truth is available to anyone anywhere. When we open God's Word, we hear Yahweh speak—the personal God of the Hebrew people who declared his existence to them so many centuries ago.

I knew nothing about this stranger in the airport except that we looked alike and had the same taste in books. Our paths crossed in a moment of time, and I'll probably never see him again. However, the memory of that encounter lives in my mind because of its significance.

God's Word will stand forever. It is more than an Old and New Testament compiled into sixty-six books that constitute a divine library. It is a source of guidance, strength, encouragement, and comfort, available every day of our lives. From the ancient sands of Israel to the shores of the New World, the Bible always has been an incredible story of faith and sacrifice. Even when it was banned, burned, and barred from the reading public, God's truth could not be crushed or stopped.

The other night I picked up *Psalms*, and as I was reading, I thought of the bearded rabbi. I remembered the day in the airport and the sweetness of that scene. I wondered if he was somewhere reading the same words as I:

> *God, teach me lessons for living*
> *so I can stay the course.*
> *Give me insight so I can do what you tell me—*
> *My whole life one long, obedient response.*
> *Guide me down the road of your commandments;*
> *I love traveling this freeway!*

(PSALM 119:33–35, *The Message*)

Take a few minutes today to spend with Yahweh. Find the comfort and guidance you need from God's words of direction for that disturbing circumstance in your life. His words are there, and they're written *just for you*.

"You are the God of Abraham, Isaac, and Jacob, and you are no less my God today than you were for them. Thank you for your provision when I need it most. Thank you for thinking of everything. Help my life be 'one long, obedient response.' Amen."

Saving Grace
Sheila Walsh

Therefore, since we have been justified through faith,
we have peace with God through our Lord Jesus Christ,
through whom we have gained access by faith into this
grace in which we now stand.

ROMANS 5:1–2

*G*race. It's a beautiful word, but I've struggled most of my life to wrap my heart around grace while trying to be perfect. Of course, perfection isn't the path to grace at all. Instead, attempted perfection (the only kind we can achieve) moves us further away from grace rather than toward it.

> *I wanted to be strong, the kind of girl you'd smile upon*
> *I wanted to be known and yet I always stood alone*
> *Holding back my fears and questions.*
> *Scared to bring them to your door.*
> *Longing for your love and kindness.*
> *But so afraid you needed more.*
> *I tried to win your heart. I always did more than my part.*
> *I tried to entertain, to make sure that you knew my name.*
> *Till finally the image crumbled and left me bleeding at your feet*
> *And in the dust of all my trying I was at the mercy seat.*
> *Saving grace*
> *You are my saving grace*
> *I'm falling down on my face*
> *Covered by saving grace*
> *Saving grace*
> *You are my saving grace*
> *Jesus, you took my place*

So I can live by saving grace
I'll never understand this gift of love that's in your hand
That asks for nothing more than "Bring your tired soul to
*   my door.*
And I will carry all your sorrow. I will let you rest awhile.
I will dress you in white linen so come to me, my darling child."
Saving grace
You are my saving grace
I'm falling down on my face
Covered by saving grace
Saving grace
You are my saving grace
Jesus, you took my place
And now I live by saving grace.
And when they ask me who am I to stand and look so strong
I'll smile and tell them I am weak, it's you I'm standing on.
Saving grace
You are my saving grace
I'm falling down on my face
Covered by saving grace
Saving grace
You are my saving grace
Jesus, you took my place
And now I live by saving grace.

Grace is a word that's so easy to say but so hard to grasp.
It's the heart of the gospel. It's the whole point. It tells us there
is nothing we can do and at the same time tells us it's already
all been done.

Nothing in my hand I bring
Simply to thy cross I cling.

I'm struck by how hard it is for so many women to embrace
grace. It's just too good to be true, especially since all the love

we experience on this earth is flawed. But grace says, "You're not okay, and I'm not okay, but that's okay." It's okay because of Jesus.

We need a long time to let this ridiculously good news sink in. Sit with it for a while. Look at yourself in the mirror and remind yourself you are completely loved and accepted by God as you are right now, not as you would like to be, but as you are. That's saving grace!

"Father in heaven, thank you for the love that reached down to save me. Thank you for the grace that is here each day to save me. Teach me to love you not out of fear but out of a broken, grateful heart. Amen."

Bridging the Gap
Patsy Clairmont

❌♥❌♥❌♥❌♥❌♥❌♥❌♥❌♥❌♥❌♥

For I am convinced that neither death nor life, neither
angels nor demons, neither the present nor the future, nor
any powers, neither height nor depth, nor anything else in
all creation, will be able to separate us from the love of
God that is in Christ Jesus our Lord.

ROMANS 8:38–39

I love to tour other people's homes. Actually, I love to tour
other people's lives. And I have been known to be an incessant interviewer with those whom I meet along life's way. Sometimes my interviewees seem a tad reluctant, but I don't dis-
courage easily. Because of this tell-me-all-you-know gene of
mine, I even enjoy snooping through other's homes and lives
on the TV Home and Garden channel.

On a recent program, a well-seasoned Michigan couple
showed their lovely 1800s restored home. What really caught
my attention was an activity they were involved in that was
casually mentioned. Each morning at 6:30 this duo sets off on
a frisky jaunt to prepare for the traditional walk across the
Mackinac Bridge, which they have been taking part in for years.

The dedicated pair pace off two-and-a-half miles each morning for months prior to Memorial Day (bridge day) to build their
stamina. In fact, they were so consistent in their practice walks
that neighbors could set their clocks by the couple. By the time
the holiday arrived, they were ready to join thousands of other
folks for the big crossing.

One reason this couple captured my attention is because
I'm a rousing Michigan native. Yeah, Michigan! But more
importantly, I have a deep appreciation for that bridge because

it led me and kept me connected to Les prior to our marriage. I lived in a suburb of Detroit in the bottom of the Lower Peninsula, and Les lived in a tiny town at the top of the Upper Peninsula. The Mackinac Bridge united the Upper and Lower Peninsulas, and us. Yeah, bridge!

Since marrying, Les and I have crossed the Mackinac Bridge more than a hundred times on our treks to visit family. We too traverse the expanse via foot—that's with Les's right foot firmly pressed on the pedal of our van's accelerator. We have often scurried across the five-mile bridge in anticipation of seeing family on the other side.

This famous bridge arches over the spot where Lakes Huron and Michigan merge. If you throw a quarter over one side, your money will be deposited in the Huron while a coin off the other side ends up officially in Lake Michigan. Hmm, the bridge brought together two lakes, two peninsulas, two sweethearts, and two families. No wonder I'm fond of this stretch of metal girders, cables, and highway.

An even greater expanse separates earth and heaven. Christ became our bridge to God. Christ offers us daily assistance, divine opportunities, and eternal provision. He also extends to us his Word, which allows us to arch over this world's distorted mind-set to receive the pure wisdom that is from above.

Speaking of bridges, what about prayer? In quiet conversations with our Lord, we hear in our longing hearts of his expansive love, which helps us to move from our inner conflict to his peaceful resolution.

As if that weren't enough, he allows people who are sometimes as disconnected from each other as two peninsulas to be united by the bridge of forgiveness.

What gap yawns before you? What provision has God made to span that distance and to bring together that which has been separated by sin, time, and emotional distance? What do you need to do to avail yourself of that provision?

"Dear Lord, thank you for bridging heaven and earth, for without you our feet of clay would be stuck in earth's mire. Tour our hearts even if we seem reluctant, and help us to be faithful bridge walkers. In fact, Lord, wouldn't it be something if others could set their watches by our daily exemplary lives? May we show that kind of dedication and preparation. We realize that one day—one memorable day—we will finally cross over to the other side to be eternally united with you. To that we say, 'Yeah, Lord!' Amen."

Over and Above What We Dreamed

God's Surprises

xvxvxvxvxvxvxvxvxvxvxvxv

Help, Lord, There's a Cat on My Face

Sheila Walsh

I lift up my eyes to the hills—where does my help come from? My help comes from the LORD, the Maker of heaven and earth. He will not let your foot slip—he who watches over you will not slumber; indeed, he who watches over Israel will neither slumber nor sleep.

PSALM 121:1–4

With all my years of traveling, I've slept in some strange places. My great comfort when I'm far away from home is that the Lord never sleeps but watches over me whether I'm in Bangkok, Britain, or Boise, Idaho.

Some of the most powerful memories are from my time as a youth evangelist in Europe. In Britain, an evangelist or singer would never stay in a hotel after an evening meeting. Hospitality—and I use that word advisedly—would be extended from a member of the local church. That hospitality is what drove me to lift my eyes to my sleepless God to extend his help.

I remember staying with an old lady in Bristol, England, who had forty-three cats. I like cats, but forty-three are about forty-two cats too many for me. I drank my cup of cocoa with cat fur in it, and then thanked my hostess and headed to bed.

"My little darlings will follow you!" she sang out after me.

I turned to see a plague of fur flow after me. "That's all right," I said. "I can find my room."

"It's where my darlings sleep, too!" She smiled as she delivered this good news.

Fluffy, Muffy, and the gang made themselves comfortable on the bed, in my suitcase, and in my toilet bag. We were a family.

As I went to sleep I prayed, "Lord, please keep these beasts off me while I'm sleeping."

I woke up to find I was suffocating. I must be in a cave, a tunnel, I was drowning . . . no, it was worse than that. "Help, Lord, there's a cat on my face!"

Another town, another trauma. The couple who took me home after church seemed very nice and almost normal. As we pulled into the driveway of their home, I listened, but not a bark or a purr could be heard. Peace!

After supper the lady asked me if I minded sleeping in the garage. I said that was fine, assuming they had converted it into some sort of bedroom. But the man of the house pulled his car out of the garage and unfolded a camp bed in its place. It was November in England and very cold. I put on more clothes to go to bed than I had on during the day. (Where are forty-three cats when you need them?) Every thirty minutes the freezer would start up and *chug, chug* till I longed for a cat to put in each ear.

In the morning, as I lay there stiff from cold and discomfort, the husband started his car to go to work, and all the exhaust came flooding in. I thought, *I bet they're closet atheists, and they're trying to kill me!*

I stayed with a family in Holland for a week. They spoke no English, and I spoke no Dutch. The family shouted at me the whole time, apparently thinking it would make it easier for me to understand them.

I have lots of fun stories to tell and laugh about in the comfort of my own home. But every story is held together by the common thread of God's faithfulness through it all. He was my constant companion.

Is it ever hard for you to close your eyes at night? Do you worry about what tomorrow will hold or if you will be safe until morning? Psalm 121 makes it clear God never closes his eyes. He is always watching over you ... even if you have fur in your mouth.

"Lord, thank you that you are with me as I lay down to sleep. Thank you that I am never alone, for you are with me through the darkest night. In Jesus' name. Amen."

Through It All

Marilyn Meberg

✗♥✗♥✗♥✗♥✗♥✗♥✗♥✗♥✗♥✗♥✗♥

Even though I walk through the valley ...

PSALM 23:4

*O*ne of my favorite words in the English language is *through*. I love it not for the way it sounds (like a muffled cough) or the way it looks (like two hills with a valley slung in between them), but for its meaning. It means "from beginning to end." That conveys encouragement to me.

It's not at all like the word *stuck*. *Stuck* sounds unattractive and feels discouraging. "It's a shame your tongue is stuck in that Coke bottle ... hang on, and I'll get my slingshot." "You just missed the only flight out. I guess you're stuck here in Odorville for the next two days." "So sorry you didn't see the wet cement sign ... You seem to be pretty well stuck."

Only last week the implications of *through* encouraged me as I valiantly tried to organize my records for Russ, my tax man. The job really shouldn't be that difficult, but I'm not a detail person, and I do pack around a numbers phobia. That adds up to a challenge.

For one thing, I'm in great need of a few write-offs. Since I'm a widow with no dependents, I suggested to Russ that perhaps it would be to my tax advantage to marry a man with a severely damaged liver who has fourteen physically challenged offspring who require daily physical therapy. That must have been a bad idea because Russ didn't pick up on it.

At any rate, I had been searching in vain for my new computer and printer's receipts. (My old computer held such undisguised animosity toward me I simply had to terminate the relationship and start a new one.) I needed the receipts as proof for at least some teeny write-off but couldn't find them. Of course I had receipts for my new air conditioner as well as the Teledyne Water Pic showerheads for the bathrooms.

Comfort came as I nestled in with the word *through*. "Marilyn, you will get through all this muddle ... you are not stuck here ... this experience has an end ... you just aren't there yet!"

Last weekend I was flying back to Palm Desert from Chicago and made the mistake of asking my seat partner if she had had a good weekend. For more than three hours I heard about her sister-in-law's insensitivity, her husband's childlike dependence on his mother, the irresponsible way he handles money, his ex-wife's whining demands, and my seat partner's increasingly severe colitis. She leaned in closer and closer to me with each revelation, and I leaned farther and farther into the aisle. But one painful encounter with the beverage cart threw me back into place quickly.

I don't normally mind these kinds of encounters—even though the woman barely came up for a breath the entire trip. But I was especially fatigued that day and found myself lacking the emotional stamina to keep a good attitude about her relentless negativity. What encouraged my spirits was the knowledge that ultimately I would get through the trip ... I wasn't stuck with this woman forever.

For years my spirits have been buoyed by the concept of the word *through*, but I learned an even deeper understanding during my husband, Ken's, battle with cancer. I had promised him that he would not die in a hospital but that every effort would be made for him to remain at home. I determined to walk through every phase of that final journey with him.

On the morning he died, our daughter, Beth, and I were on either side of his bed, literally talking him into eternity. But what struck me as he took his final breath was that I could walk only so far through the experience with him. Earthbound limits were placed on me. I was, in essence, stuck here.

Psalm 23 says, "Even though I walk through the valley of the shadow of death, I will fear no evil, for you are with me." The only one able to walk through the valley with Ken was the Shepherd. The eternal truth, "You are with me," can be ascribed only to God.

I find that truth comforting. Yes, the word *through* means there will be an end to whatever is happening with me on this earth. But an even greater promise in that word is that, when God walks me through, he suffers no human limitation; there is no separation from him. While God is with me in all my earthly "throughs," I'm heading for that final walk through, and we're doing it together!

"The promise, Lord, of your continual and unfailing presence with me as I walk through the challenges of life restores and encourages my soul. Thank you for providing that which no one else can. Only you can see me through. Help me today to do just that. Amen."

Masterpiece
Patsy Clairmont

✗❤✗❤✗❤✗❤✗❤✗❤✗❤✗❤✗❤✗❤✗❤

He who began a good work in you will carry it on to
completion until the day of Christ Jesus.

PHILIPPIANS 1:6

One of the featured art pieces at the J. Paul Getty Museum
in Los Angeles is *Prayerbook for a Queen: The Hours of
Jeanne d'Evreux*. This tiny, artistic masterpiece, on loan to the
museum, was a gift to the queen of France seven hundred years
ago. Only three-and-a-half inches high by two-and-a-half
inches wide, the prayer book consists of painted vellum pages.
Part of what distinguishes the Getty display is that the book's
leaves have been removed from the binding to photograph each
page, allowing nearly sixty pages to be displayed for public viewing as opposed to the usual two. Two dozen full-scale illumi-
nations from the book, done by miniaturist Jean Pucelle, are
now visible for museum-goers.

Imagine having your prayer book considered historical and
worthy of people lining up to view it. Today many of us keep
tabs on our prayer lives through journals in which we write
our concerns, feelings, and activities, culminating in a prayer
that might be two lines or two pages long. Some of us diligently
keep both a life journal, in which we record life's events and
our feelings, and a prayer journal, which consists of our requests
and praises offered up to our Father.

Now, I stated that as if to suggest I do, which isn't accu-
rate. I'm an occasional scribbler of thought and prayer, not a
daily one. Oh, I pray daily; I just don't record daily. In fact,
for years my personal scribbles were done on the backs of

envelopes, napkins, and old receipts. Wouldn't that be great museum fodder? They could be displayed in a bushel basket. Perhaps they could be called "Patsy's Paltry Prayers." Although, good news, today I have advanced to a leather journal. My last entry, though, was two months ago; so you don't have to worry about my trying to send you on any guilt trip. (I'd have to buy my own ticket first.)

Luci, on the other hand, has kept exquisite journals for years. Hers truly are worthy of public viewing—if they weren't so personal. She is an artist with an eye for placement, and her printing is elegant. Her own art (sketches, watercolors, colored pencil) dots the landscape of her journals as do photographs and other memorabilia. Perhaps seven hundred years from now (surely Jesus will come for us before then), Luci's work, like the queen's, will be carefully offered for public scrutiny. I know I would line up to see it. (I would be only 753 years old.)

As I considered the queen's book, I couldn't help thinking about the King's book, the Bible. Now there is a journal if I ever saw one. Talk about exquisite, have you read David's psalms lately? Open up to a page and read afresh the sweet songs of a young shepherd, hear the cries of a pursued warrior, and the anguish of a repentant king. From the pause in pastures, to pleas for pardon, to peals of praise, the account is David's journey; it's his prayer book. Amazingly enough, it's available for public viewing.

Talk about art, the Song of Solomon, the book of Ruth, and the creation account paint vivid pictures on the canvas of our hearts. Each word from the Scriptures, like brush-strokes, allows us breathtaking views all the way from Mount Nebo, to Calvary, to the Emmaus Road, and finally to the crystal river flowing from God's throne. The prophetic utterances of Ezekiel, Daniel, and Revelation render art almost beyond our imagining. And don't miss the musings of King Solomon in the Proverbs, Hagar's heartrending struggles, the eloquence of the Sermon on the Mount, or Paul's dramatic shipwrecks.

Imagine all of this and more—much, much more. No waiting in line to view this life-changing masterpiece. In fact, if your home is like mine, you have several choices of Bibles. Let's not let them become museum pieces or dust collectors. Instead, let's daily invest ourselves in the pages that we might become true works of art at the hands of the Creator.

"Dear Author and Finisher of our faith, thank you that you will complete the (art) work you have begun in us. May you transform us into pleasing renderings of your exquisite beauty. Amen."

He Knows My Name

Luci Swindoll

❌❤❌❤❌❤❌❤❌❤❌❤❌❤❌❤❌❤❌❤

The watchman opens the gate for him, and the sheep
listen to his voice. He calls his own sheep by name and
leads them out.

JOHN 10:3

The minute I saw the book I started dreaming. When Dr. Billy Graham's autobiography, *Just as I Am*, was published, I longed to give a leather-bound copy to my friend Ney Bailey. Ney had trusted the Lord with Dr. Graham during the 1951 Shreveport, Louisiana, Crusade. Not just her spiritual father, Dr. Graham is also one of her heroes in the faith. I could think of nothing more delightful than for her to receive a copy of his book, personally inscribed by him to her.

So my quest began. I wanted it for a Christmas present, and I went after it like Indiana Jones pursued the lost ark.

First I wrote Zondervan Publishing to obtain a leather-bound edition. Then I called Dr. Graham's office. The book came quickly, but I received no response to my call for an autograph. I wrote a letter explaining how desperate I felt and how important this was. Four months passed. Nothing! I wrote again. Finally, a very sweet letter of apology came, advising me there would be no autograph due to Billy Graham's ill health and his busy schedule. The unsigned book was enclosed.

I was crushed. Tempted to give up, I kept thinking, *It's not over till it's over. And, Lord, it ain't over!*

Less than a week later, I was having dinner with friends. We were engaged in enjoyable conversation about nothing in particular when Sheila Walsh casually mentioned her friend Ruth Graham.

Ruth Graham? I thought. *As in . . . Billy Graham?* I was quiet, but my heart raced. Maybe my friend Sheila could lead me to the Holy Grail. "Ahem, Sheila," I said casually, "not to change the subject, but how well do you know Ruth Graham?"

Sheila popped back in her Scottish brogue, "She's one of my best friends. I'm *nuts* about 'er."

I took a deep breath, trying to contain my excitement. Then I explained the whole thing to Sheila. "Give me the book," she said, "I'll see wha' I cun do."

She went right to work on it, sending the book with a personal note to Billy Graham. I prayed.

Three weeks passed. Nothing! *Then . . .* just before I was to be with Ney for Christmas, Sheila called, yelling into the phone, "Luci, the book came. It's wonderful. Listen to what he said . . ." It was incredible. Sheila cried. I cried. And everybody who had been praying cried.

But *nobody* cried like Ney. When Christmas morning came and she unwrapped that book, the tears began. They continued as she read aloud:

"To Ney Bailey,
God bless you always.
Billy Graham.
Philippians 1:6."

Ney exclaimed, "He knows my name! He knows my *name!*" It was an enormously gratifying moment worth all the waiting.

Philippians 1:6 says, "He who began a good work in you will carry it on to completion." That was such a reality to us that day. God had begun his work in Ney's young heart in the Shreveport stadium years ago. Through the years, he had been faithful to continue. Ney had grown. And been used by him to lead thousands to Christ.

I was reminded through the whole scenario with the book that God is interested in the tiniest things in the world. He cares about us and what we consider important. He gives us the desires of our hearts. He completes what he begins. He knows us by name.

"Lord, how I praise you for seeing us through to the end. You ask us to trust you. You call us by name. What a joy it is that you know us personally. Amen."

Payday
Thelma Wells

The man who plants and the man who waters have one
purpose, and each will be rewarded according to his
own labor.

1 CORINTHIANS 3:8

One of the sweet benefits of speaking for the Women of Faith
conferences is receiving a candy bar. Often, but not always,
Mary Graham, the program coordinator, gives each speaker a Payday candy bar for keeping her presentation within the allotted
time. Sometimes she gives us one just because she cares.

I think she's smart not to hand them out each conference
because we've begun to expect them. We're like little children.
We ooh and ah over our Paydays more than we do our paychecks—well, almost more. Getting that candy bar with "Payday" written on the wrapper ignites a spark of joy in us.

I wonder how it will be when we Christians are around
Christ's judgment seat, and he's looking over our record at the
assignments he has given us while we were on earth. He will
be handing out Paydays, too. Well, actually he calls them
"crowns" or "rewards." Five crowns will be available to us if we've
followed his orders. Five crowns? Yes! And I want all of them.

True, no amount of work will enable you to inherit eternal
life. The plan of salvation is simply to believe Jesus is Lord
and that God raised him from the dead. Salvation is a gift.

But works count for something. Ain't that good news! James
1:12 says, "Blessed is the man who perseveres under trial,
because when he has stood the test, he will receive the *crown
of life* that God has promised to those who love him."

"Do you not know that in a race all the runners run, but only one gets the prize? . . . Everyone who competes in the games goes into strict training. They do it to get a crown that will not last; but we do it to get a *crown that will last forever* [an imperishable crown]" (1 Corinthians 9:24–25).

"For what is our hope, our joy, or the *crown in which we will glory in the presence of our Lord Jesus* [a crown of exultation] when he comes? Is it not you? Indeed, you are our glory and joy" (1 Thessalonians 2:19–20).

"But you, keep your head in all situations, endure hardship, do the work of an evangelist, discharge all the duties of your ministry. For I am already being poured out like a drink offering, and the time has come for my departure. I have fought the good fight, I have finished the race, I have kept the faith. Now there is in store for me the *crown of righteousness*, which the Lord, the righteous Judge, will award to me on that day— and not only to me, but also to all who have longed for his appearing" (2 Timothy 4:5–8).

"Be shepherds of God's flock that is under your care, serving as overseers—not because you must, but because you are willing, as God wants you to be; not greedy for money, but eager to serve; not lording it over those entrusted to you, but being examples to the flock. And when the Chief Shepherd appears, you will receive the *crown of glory* that will never fade away" (1 Peter 5:2–4). (This crown is not just for pastors but for all those who are faithful to whatever ministry God has called them.)

I'm excited just thinking about that pageant of crowns I can qualify for if I work the works of him who sent me. Just like speaking at the Women of Faith conferences. I work because I know God has placed me there, not to receive that Payday candy bar. But when Mary hands me that sweet slab, I cherish it. In a much deeper way, I will cherish that last chance to be rewarded for a life well spent when I receive my rewards in heaven.

Do you like to receive gifts? Maybe nobody will recognize your works on earth, but God will never forget what you've done for him. He sees your heart and knows your motives. You, too, can look forward to your Payday in heaven.

"Father, I'm amazed to think that you will judge us Christians for things we've done for you. If our works are genuine, they are made of gold, silver, and precious stones. If not, they are like wood, hay, straw. Gracious Lord, sometimes I'm negligent and don't even think about the good I could do—not to be rewarded but because you knew it would satisfy my longing to participate in life. Please, Lord, accept my apology for not always following your instructions. Help me to remember that you have many crowns to set on my head in the hereafter, but keep me mindful of doing good not for payday but for you. Amen."

Honey, Did We Shrink-Wrap the Kids?

Barbara Johnson

He will ... save the children of the needy.

PSALM 72:4

I think of kids as people who spread peanut butter, measles, and happiness. They start out as babies, totally dependent on you, the lucky parents, for everything from food to clothing. Then they end up as teenagers, old enough to dress themselves at last—that is, if they could just remember where they dropped their clothes. How is a mom supposed to know how to relate to these fluctuating personalities?

I think raising little ones is like looking in a mirror: We get the best results when we smile. Grin more, not less. Lighten up. Let stuff go. Don't try to be supermom. Do what you do well and leave the rest to God.

Hugs help, too. Seize the day, the hour, the moment—to tickle, cavort, and celebrate your children! After all, you have a treasure at your dining table, in front of the TV, out on the baseball field, or attached to those headphones. Always be your kids' biggest fan. Cheer your kids on. Then chill out. Remember, the best way to proceed through the parenting process is to pray, "Dear Lord, please put your arm around my shoulder and your hand over my mouth."

Of course, kids grow up unpredictably. Sometimes they don't turn out like we expected. They may do things that bring us shame. Or they may die before we do. All of them wrestle with tough issues, the likes of which we never imagined. If we could shrink-wrap them to protect them from the world, we would. Instead, we tell them we hope they find contentment and God's love. We let them go. Then, when they fall back our way, we catch them and try not to act too surprised.

The Bible talks a lot about kids. One of the first references is the pain with which we bring them into the world (Genesis 3:16). In one of the last Scriptures, the apostle whom Jesus loved wrote, "I have no greater joy than to hear that my children are walking in the truth" (3 John 4). There you have it: pain intertwined with joy.

In between these references are scores of other verses, each with a story to tell. Right in the middle, the psalmist reminds us that children are a reward from the Lord (Psalm 127:3). Let's not forget that for a moment!

Let's also remember that kids are not yet what they should be. Nor are they yet what they are going to be. But then, they are not what they were. They are on their way—thanks to you, who touched their lives so significantly.

And it goes the other way, too. The highest reward for parents' toil is not what we get for it, but what we become by it. We grow and stretch and get pulled. We lose our starch. We become comfortable with ourselves. With others. And with other people's kids, which is good because eventually, by God's design, we are recycled. We become grandparents. And grandparents are the best kind of baby-sitters; they actually watch the kids rather than the TV.

But don't forget, whatever else you do, be nice to your kids. They'll choose your nursing home!

"Dear Father, thank you for my wonderful kids! (Or help me to see how wonderful they really are.) Bless every day we have together. And I will bless them in your name. Amen."

When Words Matter

Luci Swindoll

Listen, O heavens, and I will speak; hear, O earth, the
words of my mouth. Let my teaching fall like rain and my
words descend like dew, like showers on new grass, like
abundant rain on tender plants.

DEUTERONOMY 32:1–2

All I wanted was something to take off the chill. I was in
the Cincinnati airport with my dear friend Ann Wright.
Feeling rather cold, I suggested, "How 'bout a nice cup of hot
chocolate?" We headed toward a little coffee bar I'd spotted
when we deplaned.

We moseyed over to the counter and asked the woman for
two cups of hot chocolate. With a smile she said, "We don't
serve hot chocolate here, ma'am, but right over there you'll find
some. Ask for 'Christine Miller.' They're the best."

Now, I heard *nothing* about Christine Miller. But that was
exactly what Ann swears she heard. *I* felt sure the waitress
encouraged us to *"ask for skim milk."* Since my companion was
older, wiser, and more experienced, I took her word for it.

Ann found a table for two as I ordered two Christine Millers.
"Christine *what?*" was the incredulous response.

"Christine Millers! I understand that's the best hot chocolate. Two please."

Well, you should have seen the blank expression on that
poor woman's face. She verbally stumbled around, drew back
from the counter, peered underneath in search of something,
and finally responded, "I'm sorry, ma'am. All we have is Carnation." I felt sure she thought we had already been drinking
somewhere else.

Holding back my laughter, I muttered, "That's fine. I'll take it; no problem" and went to find the perpetrator of this whole mess. There she sat, patiently waiting for her Christine Miller. I hated to tell her she was having a plain old Carnation hot chocolate!

Ann and I have laughed about that for months. We've told it to others with relish. Who cares if clerks in the Cincinnati airport consider us complete idiots? No harm done. The joke was on us. As I've heard Gloria Gaither say, "Don't hear what I say . . . hear what I mean."

Wouldn't *that* be great? Sometimes, though, our words are of utmost importance. Saying the right thing is crucial.

Last Christmas I was cruising along the Chilean coast, when suddenly we spotted a wrecked ship jutting out of the water, high and dry. The captain informed us this was the "Santa Leonora" which, on her maiden voyage in 1964, went aground due to a misunderstood command. The captain and the helmsman had been engaged in conversation when they transited "shoal pass." On completion of their talk, the captain simply said, "Alright, pilot." The pilot responded with a full right rudder, causing the ship to veer sharply to starboard and mount the shallows at full speed, where she still rests today. The captain had said a casual, "alright," but the pilot had heard the instruction, "all right," which meant something very different. The result was deadly.

God speaks to us clearly. He means what he says. When he says he'll provide, we can count on that. When he promises peace, wisdom, strength, or comfort, they are ours. God imparts his word and keeps it. His words matter! I find tremendous comfort in that.

Sit down with a cup of hot chocolate today and enjoy his Word. Try a Christine Miller, alright?

"Help me to believe you completely, Lord. Remind me you are never confused or distracted, but what you say you mean. Reveal in my own life the truth of this every day so my faith gets stronger and stronger. Amen."

Firsthand Knowledge
Thelma Wells

No temptation has seized you except what is common to
man. And God is faithful; he will not let you be tempted
beyond what you can bear. But when you are tempted, he
will also provide a way out so that you can stand up under it.

1 CORINTHIANS 10:13

In March 1998, Luci and I spoke at a church conference
near Dallas with the theme of friendship. Luci spoke on
friendships with others. I was asked to speak on friendship with
Jesus. At first I thought, *This is a breeze.* Then I started to figure out how to approach the subject.

I asked God to give me what he wanted me to say. Nothing
happened. The time drew nearer, and I kept thinking and thinking, jotting down ideas, trying to get it together. Nothing made
sense. The afternoon before the conference, still nothing had
come. About 9:30 the night before, God came through. (Why
can't he be early sometimes?) This is what occurred to me.

Have you ever considered that Jesus the God-man experienced everything we humans experience? I can see him as a
baby crying, kicking, scooting, crawling, pulling up, learning
how to eat and walk just like an ordinary baby. As a little toddler, Jesus played and got dirty. Mary and Joseph would tell him
to stop doing little toddler things and try to get him to put his
food in his mouth—and leave it there.

I can see Jesus' earthly father instructing him in carpentry.
I can imagine Jesus playing outside with the neighborhood kids
and his parents telling him to come inside at a certain time.
When Jesus got left behind in Jerusalem, I can imagine Mary,
after missing him, saying to the other children, "Have you all

seen Jesus? I thought he was walking with you. You mean none of you has seen him since we left the temple? Oh, my goodness, we have to go back and find that boy." They, of course, found him in the temple going about his Father's business.

Can't you see him at mealtime listening attentively to Jewish history and learning Jewish customs? Parents were to teach their children in the morning, afternoon, evening, and night. As the older people discussed the Law, can't you just see this inquisitive boy straining his ears to hear every word?

He had the same physical needs that we have. He got hungry and thirsty. He grew tired and needed to rest and go on vacation like we do. He showed emotions. He wept and became angry and disgusted. He enjoyed a good party. He motivated crowds of people. He enjoyed recreation. He was tested. He understood fear and sadness. He was surrounded with rebellion and death. He dealt with sickness and disease. He was unacknowledged in his hometown. He was ridiculed and talked about, lied to and left out. He was falsely accused and abused and experienced prejudice. He was humiliated, beaten, and killed.

Jesus is the only friend who understands everything that can happen to us. He knows firsthand how situations feel, taste, smell, sound, hurt, tempt, disappoint, excite, motivate, influence, stimulate ... everything. We can feebly try to tell him about our experiences, but he already knows, sees, and understands.

A favorite hymn of mine says:

Jesus is all the world to me.
My life. My joy. My all.
He is my strength from day to day.
Without him I would fall.
When I am sad, to him I go.
No other one can cheer me so.
When I am sad
He makes me glad.
He's my friend.

"Jesus, you experienced the good, the bad, and the ugly. A thought can't even slip through my mind that you haven't already known. You see the before, during, and after of every event. When I think that you physically, mentally, and spiritually tasted all of my experiences, it's easier for me to rely on you for direction, clarity, instruction, healing, emotional stability, spiritual growth, and wisdom. Thank you, Jesus, for being my friend. Amen."

Stargazing

Barbara Johnson

✖♥✖♥✖♥✖♥✖♥✖♥✖♥✖♥✖♥✖♥✖♥
Delight yourself in the LORD and
he will give you the desires of your heart.

PSALM 37:4

A crippled old man hobbled on the beach at low tide, picking up stranded starfish and throwing them back into the sea. A boy saw him and asked, "Why are you doing that? What a waste of time!" When the old man explained that starfish die if left in the sun, the boy replied, "But there are thousands of beaches and millions of stranded starfish. You think you're making a difference?"

The old man bent over to pick up another starfish. Flinging it back into the sea, he said, "I am to this one!"

God encourages us to make ourselves and our desires—however insignificant they seem—available for his kingdom work. Spiritual leaders aren't necessarily those with a high profile. They are the ones who put their personal dreams to work to make life better for someone else. They translate desire into service because they believe that desire is a gift from God himself.

What about you? What is your dream? What do you deeply desire? Could it be that those desires have been planted in your heart by the heavenly Father? Do you believe he has a purpose for your most cherished dream because it originated with him? God wants you to pursue the talents he has created within you. He means for them to blossom through your personality. Your availability makes it happen.

Each one of us has ideas spinning in her heart and head. They are there for a reason. If we allow our desires to be purified by the Holy Spirit, fueled by the light of Christ, and warmed by our passion for God's will, we will make a difference in this world.

But what about our broken dreams or long-unfulfilled desires? One woman was propelled into writing when her husband died. "Even when you have a wound so big you can drive a truck through it," she said, "you don't have the luxury to give up on your dreams." She wrote to bless others.

Last week I saw this bumper sticker on a passing car, "My karma just ran over my dogma!" Maybe you think because something bad has run over your precious dreams you have the right to give up on God and your hopes. "What use is it, anyway?" you ask. "How can I possibly get over disappointment and keep going?"

The process you go through to deal with a lost dream includes these steps. First, you *churn*. You feel like your insides are being processed in a grinder. That's okay; you're being honest.

Second, you *burn*. You are full of anger and frustration. That's okay; God is doing his work in you.

Third, you *yearn*. You want things to be the way they were before they went wrong. You want your circumstances to change. (This stage lasts the longest.) That's okay; just hang on.

Fourth, you *learn* that desire boomerangs. You can restore your loss by giving love, hope, a helping hand, a little money, and a lot of compassion.

Last, you *turn* the problem over to God. Say, "Whatever, Lord. You are big enough to get me through this."

How do you keep believing, keep the faith, keep the spiritual workout up? By knowing God hasn't given up on you! He has never lost faith. He sees the dream in your heart as bright as the lights on a Broadway marquee. Not one ounce of his enthusiasm for your talents has dissipated.

It also helps to know that God is big enough to handle your doubts, slumps, and temper tantrums. He is staying in your court. He isn't going to drop the ball in your game of life. And he is your biggest fan!

Someone once wrote me, "Sometimes I'm up; sometimes I'm down. I wish I could bottle feeling good and take a dose when I'm down." Not a single one of us has the luxury of giving up! With God, you reenter the arena of your fear, your failing, or your fatigue. No matter how you feel, dig your toes deep right now into the truth of Psalm 37:4. God will give you your heart's desire. He said it; it's true.

I read these words in a card sent to me years ago: "It is not what seems fair, but what is true; not what we dream, but what we do." That thought is a mainstay for me as I keep on keeping on through the worst of times.

Those who have read some of my books know I've been through enough trauma to have given up throwing my "starfish" back into the sea a thousand times. I could have just said, "Enough is enough, Lord, I'm outta here." Instead, I've chosen to say, "Whatever, Lord!" In dark periods, I felt burned out, outdated, and washed out. But I hung onto the truth of God's enthusiasm for me. It set me free to follow his dream.

Insert the key to your personal dream into the door of God's kingdom-keeping bank vault. Allow God to take that which feels like defeat and turn it for good. When you do this, you haven't given up; you have displayed courage. Then God will entrust you with starfish—or help you to reach the stars.

"Heavenly Father, my personal desire is to _____ _____. I am making myself available to you. I will not give up. I want to be involved with people and with living and loving to make your kingdom come. Amen."

Lost and Found

Patsy Clairmont

❤✗❤✗❤✗❤✗❤✗❤✗❤✗❤✗❤✗❤✗❤✗❤

… Christ in you, the hope of glory.

COLOSSIANS 1:27

Keep this under your hat: Paradise Lost has been found. No kidding, Les and I have found our Shangri-La. At every turn, we see breathtaking vistas of rocky ranges, flowered borders, and peach sunsets. Palm trees dance in celebration, swishing their fronds like feather dusters in the sky. And bougainvillea cascades across the landscape, climbing, draping, and spilling down walls. A profusion of gardens, fountains, and pools bring soothing, visual refreshment. The evening sky, like a great dome, surrounds us in a spectacular display of illumination. Even the mountains daily shout strength and beauty. Ah, yes, paradise, Palm Desert, California.

I don't know about you, but I'm susceptible to viewing the lives of others from afar and believing their existence is easier, calmer, and more meaningful than mine—rather paradisiacal. Not all the time, mind you, but I do have those moments when I give way to envy because I'm trudging through a dreary season while someone else seems to be skipping down a well-lit path. But I guess peeking over the fence at the greener grass is part of our human tendency. I mean, consider some of these folks …

Sarah of Genesis fame felt God was tardy fulfilling his promises to her regarding a baby. So she thought she would assist him. Sarah had trudged through many seasons waiting for a child and had since entered midlife, which doused her fruitful hopes. But Sarah took a peek at Hagar her servant, and hark, Hagar was like a skipping roe. In Sarah's mind her sweet servant girl would be just the right choice to bear her husband's child on Sarah's behalf.

Wrong! Paradise turned into "Big-Time Wrestling" when Hagar began to tout her success and Sarah began to shout her disapproval. Sarah was offended. Abraham was saddened. And Hagar was expelled from their midst. Alas, seems Sarah was better off before she started helping God out.

King Ahab had incredible riches and power. But when he looked over the fence and saw his neighbor's yard, Ahab knew he had to own that plot of land. Why, anyone could see it was the ideal place for the king's garden. Well, almost anyone— just not the owner, who wasn't the least bit interested in selling. Ahab broke out into a big-time case of the pouts. The queen, in her attempt to give her whining husband everything he wanted (paradise), had the neighbor bumped off. But planting the seeds of disdain in any ground will only bring forth disaster. Ask King Ahab or Queen Jezebel. In fact, you may want to examine for yourself their dogged trail of regret (in 1 Kings 22:34–37 and 2 Kings 9:30–37). Hmm, if only they had been satisfied with what they already had.

Oh, yeah, about Les's and my paradise, did I mention the sand? Oh, well, it's everywhere. When the winds whip, the sand permeates the condo even though the doors and windows are closed tightly. And the winds sometimes become so vengeful it causes the entire valley to howl like a dust bowl. This winter a swirling wind tore out sixty trees near us—very near us, outside our door. Then there's the heat and lack of humidity that leaves one's body withering for moisture. And the screeching night frogs that sound like a woman's screams for help. Not to mention the black widow spiders, the legions of grasshoppers, and the earthquakes. Well, there goes paradise, lost again.

Some sand and wind will come into everyone's life, no matter how perfect it seems. Remember screaming Sarah, who was almost blown away in her attempts to have things her way. And withering Ahab, who tripped himself up when his sandals filled with another man's sandy soil.

Keep this under your hat (where your brains are) and in your heart (where hope abides): "In this life we shall have tribulations . . ." Paradise? That comes later.

"Lord, may we be grateful for all you have given us. Would you please guard our hearts against envy and from our own self-serving agendas? Thank you for the promise of a future paradise. May we wait expectantly and patiently. Amen."

FAITH

OverJoyed! is based on the popular
Women of Faith conferences.

Women of Faith is partnering with Zondervan Publishing
House, Integrity Music, *Today's Christian Woman* magazine,
and Campus Crusade to offer conferences, publications,
worship music, and inspirational gifts that support and
encourage today's Christian women.

Since their beginning in January of 1996, the Women of
Faith conferences have enjoyed an enthusiastic welcome
by women across the country. Call 1-888-49-FAITH for
the many conference locations and dates available.

See following pages for additional information
about Women of Faith products.

www.women-of-faith.com

Women of Faith Friends

Friends Through Thick & Thin

**Gloria Gaither,
Peggy Benson,
Sue Buchanan,
and Joy MacKenzie**

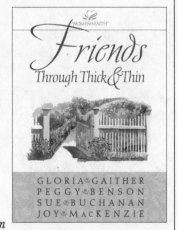

The authors, who have been good friends for over thirty years, celebrate the ups and downs and all-arounds of friendship. *Friends Through Thick & Thin* spotlights the relationships that add beauty, meaning, and sanity to our daily lives. Sit back and revel in this joyous, personal time of sharing with four extraordinary women.

Hardcover 0-310-21726-1

Deeper Joy for Your Journey

Bring Back the Joy
Sheila Walsh

Capturing the theme of the 1998 Women of Faith conferences, *Bring Back the Joy* is a warm, encouraging, and richly personal invitation to experience the joy that comes from loving and being loved by the Most Important Person in the Universe. In *Bring Back the Joy*, Sheila Walsh writes about rekindling the joy in your life and in your relationship with God. With great wisdom gained through learning and growing with other women as a key speaker at Women of Faith conferences across the nation, she calls us to a deeper joy, exposes the negative forces designed to steal our joy, and shows us how to sow life-changing seeds of joy.

Hardcover 0-310-22023-8
Audio Pages 0-310-22222-2

More for Your Joyful Journey . . .

The Joyful Journey

**Patsy Clairmont,
Barbara Johnson,
Marilyn Meberg,
and Luci Swindoll**

With trademark warmth and good humor, the authors share from their hearts and lives about the obstacles, bumps, and detours we sometimes face along the journey of life and about how friendship, laughter, and celebration can help steer our hearts closer to God.

**Softcover 0-310-22155-2
Audio Pages 0-310-21454-8**

The Joyful Journey
**Perpetual Calendar
Daybreak**

Three hundred sixty-six encouraging and inspiring excerpts from the book by Patsy Clairmont, Barbara Johnson, Marilyn Meberg, and Luci Swindoll celebrate life and bring joy and laughter every day of the year!

0-310-97282-5

Devotions for Women of Faith

Joy Breaks

**Patsy Clairmont,
Barbara Johnson,
Marilyn Meberg,
and Luci Swindoll**

Ninety upbeat devotionals that
motivate and support women
who want to renew and
deepen their spiritual commitment. These devotions illus-
trate practical ways to deepen
joy amidst all the complexities, contradictions, and
challenges of being a woman today. Women of all ages
will be reminded that any time, any day, they can
lighten up, get perspective, laugh, and cast all their
cares on the One who cares for them.

Hardcover 0-310-21345-2

Joy Breaks Daybreak™

Bring joy to your life every
day with 128 light-hearted,
inspiring, and joyful devotional excerpts from the
book *Joy Breaks*.

0-310-97287-6